PBL Simplified

Praise for *PBL Simplified*

"Traditional mindsets are difficult to overcome, but if you can get a few successful moments to highlight, the shift can occur. *PBL Simplified* and the accompanying book study are both great tools that we are utilizing to onboard staff and change mindsets. I also use components for parents who may be struggling with a new learning environment."

—Shannon Treece, Principal, Florida

"Bringing PBL to our schools can be difficult because it likely looks different than how most of us were taught. People fear things they do not understand well, especially since they have a sense of how the traditional school system can be navigated. PBL works best when implemented well with clarity and purpose. I believe *PBL Simplified* provides a practical guide to restoring what education should look like and how we will prepare learners for a world that requires more than our traditional school systems prepare them for."

—Nathan Manley, Assistant Superintendent, Missouri

"The book hits home for all teachers who have either implemented PBL or are about to. The chapters are short but effective in conveying what's necessary. Ryan provides advice only an experienced teacher would know in each step of the implementation process. The wins and fails were also helpful to see both sides of the process."

—Andrew Waterhouse, Teacher, Kentucky

"This book goes through the six phases of problem-solving and goes in length about doing Project Based Learning in your classroom. It doesn't matter your content or PBL experience, every teacher will find applicable information to better use PBL in their classroom. It is a quick read, an easy read, and a very informative read."

—Trish Burns, Teacher, Indiana

"Public education has more challenges than ever and great teaching is really hard. Project Based Learning can be the connection that synthesizes the many demands of educators into a practical instructional model. *PBL Simplified* is a how-to manual for teachers that allows them to see how they can connect rigor and relevance while also creating incredible learning experiences for their students. I've become a passionate promoter of PBL and Ryan's leadership and support helped me to grow as a person and leader."

—Jeff Spencer, Director of Title I, IV, and Secondary Schools, Indiana

"Modern education exists in a tension between the acquisition of content and the development of essential workforce skills. The Skills Gap is indeed a very real phenomenon, and Project Based Learning is the answer; but becoming an expert PBL practitioner takes a great deal of training, practice, and trial and error. *PBL Simplified* demystifies the essential processes of PBL and does so in a way that is friendly and unassuming. Shifting educational paradigms away from an antiquated and a century-old system happens at a glacial pace, but if you've picked up this book, you are on the leading edge of that change."

—Andrew Larson, Teacher and Author, Indiana

"Our current education system is not constructed in a way that allows us to equip students with the skills they will need in the future workforce, which is why Project Based Learning is so important for your classroom. *PBL Simplified* will help you figure out exactly how to take those first steps of implementing PBL into your school and classroom. *PBL Simplified* allows the reader to take on an overwhelming task and implement it in a way that is very doable for those that are new to the process so you too can watch students blossom into amazing learners by maximizing their strengths in the PBL classroom."

—Bobby Thompson, Principal, Indiana

"*PBL Simplified* is as concise and well-written as it is full of practical wisdom and guidance. Ryan shares stories of his own fails and successes in each chapter, so you can visualize each step and learn from his attempts. Approachable and clear, *PBL Simplified* will guide your practice whether you are new to PBL or you've been engaging your kids in authentic problems and solutions already."

—Betsy Peterson, Executive Director of Learning to Give

"Most people grow up in traditional educational models, and as an outlier Project Based Learning can be very difficult for people to understand, especially at first. *PBL Simplified* outlines a collaborative process of taking principals, teachers, and students all through the process of change and growth associated with transitioning to Project Based Learning. From the beginning of my PBL journey as Superintendent, Ryan Steuer and Magnify Learning were a crucial piece of our success. They provided timely professional development and personalized PBL support related to the unique needs of our district. They helped to shape our understanding of Project Based Learning."

—Jamie Bandstra, Superintendent, Michigan

PBL
SIMPLIFIED

6 Steps to Move **Project Based Learning**
from Idea to Reality

RYAN STEUER

NEW YORK

LONDON • NASHVILLE • MELBOURNE • VANCOUVER

PBL Simplified

6 Steps to Move Project Based Learning from Idea to Reality

© 2023 Ryan Steuer

Published in New York, New York, by Morgan James Publishing. Morgan James is a trademark of Morgan James, LLC. www.MorganJamesPublishing.com

Proudly distributed by Ingram Publisher Services.

For additional resources and a FREE accompanying study, please go to: www.magnifylearningin.org/pbl-simplified-book-resources.

Morgan James BOGO™

A **FREE** ebook edition is available for you or a friend with the purchase of this print book.

CLEARLY SIGN YOUR NAME ABOVE

Instructions to claim your free ebook edition:
1. Visit MorganJamesBOGO.com
2. Sign your name CLEARLY in the space above
3. Complete the form and submit a photo of this entire page
4. You or your friend can download the ebook to your preferred device

ISBN 9781631959394 paperback
ISBN 9781631959400 ebook
Library of Congress Control Number:
2022935589

Cover Design by:
Megan Dillon
megan@creativeninjadesigns.com

Interior Design by:
Christopher Kirk
www.GFSstudio.com

Morgan James is a proud partner of Habitat for Humanity Peninsula and Greater Williamsburg. Partners in building since 2006.

Get involved today! Visit MorganJamesPublishing.com/giving-back

This book is dedicated to all who live their "why"
every day in the service of others.

CONTENTS

ACKNOWLEDGMENTS

PBL Simplified is truly written on the shoulders of giants. Those giants have been the teachers who were shoulder to shoulder with me in the classroom blazing a trail for this work. Those giants have been the first group of learners who helped form the work and are now out in the world continuing the next chapter of success. Those giants have been the veteran facilitators who saw something great for kids, so they jumped in with both feet. Those giants are the new teacher reading this and dreaming a dream of better outcomes for kids. Thank you all for your work.

To my wife and kids, who traveled around the country with me spreading Project Based Learning in the very early days in a used travel trailer. These years have been full of joy, exploration, and love. Bring on adventure!

To my mom and dad, who have always allowed me options and shown me a world ready for exploration and entrepreneurial adventures.

To the Magnify Learning staff, who see PBL as a superpower and are constantly living the PBL process because they know it makes the world a better place.

To Morgan James Publishing for helping this book reach a broader audience, so it can produce better outcomes for the next generation, especially David Hancock and Emily Madison.

To my editor, Aubrey Kosa, whose expertise has brought clarity to the message. Many thanks for taking the excess vision and thoughts and making them helpful for others.

To the teachers who are on the front lines living out their "why" in the service of the learners in front of them each day. You are not alone, and you are on the right path!

FOREWORD

Our ideas about education are being rocked. Major companies are moving away from a focus on SATs, GPAs, brand-name schools, and credentials. Instead, they are looking at how this person thinks, solves problems, leads, and handles failure. Companies like Google, Apple, IBM, Costco, Nordstroms, Hilton, Whole Foods, Penguin Random House, and more have recently announced they no longer require applicants to have a college degree. They are looking for candidates who have hands-on experience and a proven track record of producing results.

What a perfect time to focus in on Project Based Learning. Ryan Steuer has both the classroom and the business world experience to be the expert on what we really want education to accomplish. Not to simply help students accumulate knowledge but to be prepared to make valuable contributions to the world in which we all live. To guide students in authentic learning experiences to discover their most important purposes and contributions to the world.

Reflect back on how "learning" took place even twenty years ago. One would spend time with the same people week after week.

Depending on where you lived, that may have included the gas station attendant, the local grocery store owner, your parents, a teacher or two, and the neighborhood kids who were your friends. "Learning" took place in school with the one teacher responsible for your class. If you were from a privileged family, you may have been lucky enough to have an Encyclopedia Britannica set in your house—opening you up to a vast amount of information. The choices after high school were clear. If you wanted an "education," you went to the place where they controlled additional information: college.

Colleges had big libraries with the books and research studies not available to the small-town students. Few people had the opportunity to go to college as it was expensive and required another four years outside the workforce. It was clear that college graduates had more access to knowledge and information and ultimately got better jobs and incomes. Thus, the apparent causation was obvious: if you wanted a better job and more income, you must memorize more and retain more information.

But what does that look like today? During the last twenty years, our access to that privileged information has changed dramatically. Most people now carry some form of a device in their pocket that provides instant access to that entire compilation of human knowledge and allows us to communicate with the intellectually and economically elite anywhere in the world. If you are a poor child from Alabama, a daughter of upper-income New York City parents, or one of eleven children in a family living as squatters in Nairobi, Kenya, you have access to that abundance of stored and daily developing information.

Academic programs have historically focused on memorization. Today, memorization is meaningless. To be successful, one must move beyond accumulation of knowledge to understanding and application. And that can be done in a wide variety of ways.

No longer is it a unique privilege to have access to that information, and no longer is it necessary to study and learn and memorize what is so instantly available. Want to know the capital of Ukraine? Simply speak the question into your phone and get the answer instantly. Need to know the square root of 3,456? It doesn't take some complicated paper process—anyone can access the answer of 58.79 immediately. This is not some gradual improvement or opportunity. This is an amazing, disruptive, transforming leap forward—with immense implications for "education."

Ryan clearly describes how Project Based Learning (PBL) is a teaching method in which students learn by actively engaging in real-world and personally meaningful projects.

How do we return to an educational model that includes actively engaging in real-world projects? We've watched as home economics and shop class have been eliminated in favor of more accumulation of knowledge and information. Even back in 60 AD, the Roman Stoic Seneca cautioned, "Far too many good brains have been afflicted by the pointless enthusiasm for useless knowledge."

As a poor farm kid, I saw school as an escape from the arduous dairy farm work required 365 days a year. To sit in a clean classroom and just complete the easy tasks for decent grades was a welcome respite from milking cows and throwing hay bales. Following high school, I opted to go to college, not as a career path, but as a socially acceptable way to leave the farm for good. I was not seeking information or application but simply an alternative to the limited economic model I observed on the farm. With a BA in Psychology from The Ohio State University I continued with the entrepreneurial ideas that had allowed graduation with no student loan debt. After a few years of experimentation, I returned to school to receive my MA in Psychology, again with no intention of making that a career path or the basis of generating income but rather a way of justifying continued study, which I did enjoy.

Having found success as an author and speaker, I returned to academia after another eighteen years to complete my doctoral studies. Those studies are valued, but I found that having the skill to generate significant income would have to be found outside the walls of the educational system.

And thus the quandary of education today. How do we balance the value of intellectual studies with the necessity of generating income to provide for our own needs and to live in abundance and generosity?

When my boys were young they were expert BMX riders. We learned about centrifugal force by building a bicycle racing track for our community. We learned about physics by building ramps and jumps that would project the riders into the air enough to provide a thrill without too much danger of crashing.

I have three granddaughters who have spent the last five years as full-time travelers with their parents. When asked, "Where do you go to school?" they reply, "Everywhere!" When asked, "Who is your teacher?" they reply, "Everyone!" Learning and application are seamless in their eyes. They have sold muffins at the farmer's market, created art that is replicated on sites like RedBubble, and raised snakes for sale, all while learning about pricing, inventory control, and marketing.

PBL Simplified is the next step in education that prepares our students for the changing world of work today. Work opportunities where they are not stymied by the Fermi problems that may be asked in an interview, such as "How many piano tuners are there in Chicago?" Questions that have no exact, quantifiable answer. Questions that require innovation and creative thinking rather than drawing on a reservoir of memorized knowledge.

As you move through the chapters of *PBL Simplified*, you will find the road map for defining and solving problems in new ways. Ways that will evoke the enthusiastic engagement of your students and parents while providing those students with the assurance of a broad spectrum of future opportunities. Opportunities to be leaders in innovation - in developing ideas that are new, in refining existing ideas, and providing solutions for the benefit of all humanity.

I commend you on taking this initiative to be an innovative educational leader. The kind of teacher who students will remember with pride thirty years from now. The kind of teacher who is a life-long learner, who exudes the joy of learning and the application of such for work that is meaningful, purposeful, and profitable.

—**Dan Miller,** author and coach *(48 Days to the Work You Love)*

INTRODUCTION

Live Your Why

*"The goal is not simply for you to cross
the finish line, but to see how many people
you can inspire to run with you."*
~ Simon Sinek

Skyler was disengaged in school for years. His only real ambition for the future was to figure out how he could find more time to skate with his friends. Skyler performed well in school at first, but then somewhere around third grade, he realized that even if you didn't do any work, you could still get two meals a day and hang out with your friends. The annoying classes didn't get in the way too much if you were quiet. But as Skyler floated along, he ran into a group of teachers doing Project Based Learning (PBL) who would disrupt his habitual underachievement.

Skyler is the learner you have right now, the one who has the ability to perform well but no desire or motivation. He is the kid who can find the error on your test but doesn't take the time to try on that same test. Or maybe you have the kid who messes up your whole thinking around grading because she doesn't do any of the homework and still aces the test—the learner who is full of potential but doesn't see it.

You just thought of a couple of names, didn't you? That is one of the great things about being an educator—all our stories have names, faces, and destinies!

Continuing Skyler's story, the generational poverty he grew up in showed him that school did not matter, giving him a lot of negative momentum. School was not something his family and friends valued, so he took the same bent toward education.

Like most teenagers in the twenty-first century, Skyler had an Instagram account. He started taking pictures of sunrises at the bus stop and posting them for anyone to see. After a while, he noticed he was getting a small following, so he decided to get a more advanced camera. It seemed he had a natural eye for beauty. He added some sophistication and effort to his Instagram feed with pictures of his buddies and nature scenes from state parks. Then, one day, *Time* magazine asked if they could feature a few of his photographs, and things started to change for Skyler. Skyler began gaining 5,000 followers a day until he reached 48,000 followers!

This is a true story. Every year, *Time* magazine features one Instagram account from each state in the country. Depending on the state, the representative is likely a photojournalist or a freelance photographer, but if you look up "*Time* Magazine Instagram 50," you'll see Skyler's account representing Indiana for a couple of years in a row when Skyler was only seventeen! Quite a way to climb for a kid whose most substantial previous ambition was to skate and hang out. Skyler now has a website where you can buy his photography, and he has sponsors like Coleman, Valvoline, and other recognizable brand names. He used education and learning to find a path to his dreams. Skyler now travels the country exploring and capturing natural moments.

I can't claim to have ever helped Skyler hold a camera, but he would tell you that the year he first experienced Project Based Learning was a significant shift for him. He discovered the importance of learning and community. Becoming a lifelong learner has served him well since he became a self-taught freelance photographer and Instagram influencer. If we had only focused on compound sentences instead of problem-solving and applying critical thinking, we would have done Skyler and many other learners a disservice. Project Based Learning can be the structure and the culture-building vehicle to help you engage your standards as you inspire learners the way you have always wanted to. You have a Skyler in your classroom waiting to be engaged and pointed toward his dreams.

Project Based Learning changes lives because it empowers learners to reach their highest potential under their own guidance and opens opportunities otherwise thought impossible. In short, PBL allows teachers to be in their sweet spot, to fulfill your real purpose behind accepting your calling as an educator. Nobody enters education wanting kids to be average or to master a standardized test. We become educators to help young people achieve new heights. We see learners who don't understand their full capability, and we want to open their eyes to their true options.

PBL is a different type of instructional model. It's hands-on and active, but it is also minds-on with time dedicated to reflection, contemplation, and problem-solving. This book is written the same way. Stay actively engaged as you read by keeping a Project Based Learning idea in mind, so you can create and revise as you go.

My caution to you is that this book is much more than simplifying the Project Based Learning process. This book is the start of your journey of analyzing and adapting your current instructional practices and mindsets. The traditional model of education with rows of desks, repetitive worksheets, and outdated textbooks creates a passivity in learners that cripples their future even if they do win the game of school by achieving good grades. Project Based Learning empowers your learners, which allows them to see themselves and the world differently. With PBL, we see learners who are ready to find their place in the world, a place where they can thrive and contribute meaningfully. They start to see the problems of their world as things to be solved, not just accepted.

And the empowerment of PBL not only changes the learner but often also the educator. You can expect to finally teach the way you have always wanted to teach, the way you saw in movies, the way that changes learners' lives, the way that the schoolwork you still remember fondly was done. Think about your most meaningful experience in school. When I ask educators from around the country what that meaningful experience was for them, they never say the five-paragraph essay they wrote in eighth grade; they always reference a project or activity that allowed them to make a difference in their surroundings and empowered them in some way.

My hope is that you will be open to finding the best way to reach *your* learners. Be selfish in that way. Take every part of this book and find out how it applies to *you* and *your* learners.

To help you visualize what this might look like in your classroom, every chapter includes the following components:

- Explanation of a major PBL pillar
- Win Story

- Fail Story
- Bottom Line
- Where to Start
- Resources
- Questions

The first set of chapters follows the PBL process, but each one can also stand alone, so feel free to either skip to a section that addresses your immediate needs or read them in order to get the big picture.

At this point, most of you have probably figured out that the current educational model (based on the Industrial Revolution) needs to shift. Google Sir Ken Robinson's YouTube video on Educational Paradigms if you want to hear more about that. The gist of it is that passive learning and compliance will only lead to excellent point-gatherers, which, as of the writing of this book, does not lead to the future we want for our learners. In the twenty-first century, no organization is looking to fill a room with thirty people who will only be asked to regurgitate information. In fact, employers routinely say they are looking for employees who can:

- Solve problems
- Communicate clearly
- Work in teams
- Think for themselves
- Work with ambition

So, we fight the apathy created by the current educational model with authenticity. As we help our learners move from apathetic to empowered through PBL Units that solve real-world problems, we give them the greatest chance to be successful in their future endeavors. It really doesn't matter if they are going to be an engineer or a package handler. The ability to learn and seek out new opportunities helps everyone.

At the beginning of the Project Based Learning movement, PBL units began with a fantastically engaging Entry Event and concluded with learners giving excellent presentations. Then toward the middle of the PBL Unit, there was this thing called "the mess in the middle" when we worked hard to help learners work in groups and learn the standards but lacked structure and process. The raw pioneering work has matured; we now have a structure and process that can be followed and replicated to make sure all learners are on a path to success. With massive room for personalization, innovation will always be part of education, but there need to be basic structures that give us room for—and even enhance—our creativity.

While the need for lifelong learners has always existed, the future is going to call all the more for problem-solving, engaged learners who can communicate and pursue their passions. Schools will likely still be hubs of content, but with content at our individual fingertips, providing learners with information is not the answer. We have all the answers we need in our pockets. The winners of the game of life are those who can use the information to achieve their own goals and apply it to help others.

"The illiterate of the 21st century will not be those who cannot read and write, but those who cannot learn, unlearn, and relearn."
~ Alvin Toffler

Marketing gurus say this book's introduction should amplify the problem, but you are already entrenched in the problem. You see learners every day who are passive, who are apathetic, and who would rather look at social media than think about achieving a dream. You are given too many new, disjointed ideas to implement, and it's all too easy to lose your passion for the craft. Project Based Learning brings the engagement you crave to your learners and a framework to your teaching that allows you to bring your initiatives together. You've been living with the problem all around you; let's get started on the solution!

For years I've started every professional development session I lead with Simon Sinek's TED Talk about the golden circle because it points us to our "why." The golden circle contends that effective communication starts from the "why," then the "how," and then the "what." In our daily conversation, we often start with the "what" and never even get to the "why" when the "why" is what empowers us. For instance, "What do you do?" is a typical introduction question. You can abide by the usual process and answer, "I am a teacher," but that allows the other person to project their idea of a teacher onto what you do. What if you changed your answer and put your "why" first?

"Because I believe kids have immense potential waiting to help the world, I inspire today's youth to be lifelong learners who look at the world as a set of problems they can help solve. I do all of this through my calling as a teacher."

Try it next time you are asked that question. Your conversation will be much more fruitful, guaranteed!

So, why Project Based Learning? And why now?

For me, Project Based Learning became a necessity after I realized that one of my learners had dropped out of high school the first semester of his freshman year. I didn't even know that was legal!

When I decided to become an educator, I left the world of industrial engineering at a Fortune 50 company so that I could save the world as an eighth-grade English teacher, but my attempts at engaging learners didn't seem to be working for them. Of course, I had stories of the rare learners doing great things, but I came into teaching to help all kids see more opportunities. I was working hard for kids, building relationships, and doing the best I knew how, but it didn't take too long for me to realize that passion and love weren't enough.

As a former engineer, my logic was simple: if what I was doing wasn't working, I should change. A colleague was already dabbling in Project Based Learning, so I jumped in. We made mistakes, and we let the learners know we made mistakes, and we all learned together. At the end of the day, the results were there. Attendance went up, discipline went down, standardized test scores rose, and my learners became learners who could solve their own problems. I was fulfilling my "why." Most educators have a similar "why." When I ask teachers across the country why they teach, they tell me things like:

- "I love seeing the light-bulb moments."
- "I want my learners to see their full potential."
- "My learners have so much potential to be awesome. I want them to know how special they are."
- "When I went to school, it wasn't good for me; I want my learners to know that they are loved and they can achieve their dreams."

We all want our learners to have the best opportunities. That may mean a two-year or four-year college for some, trade school for others, or going straight into the workforce. What we mostly want is for our learners to be happy with their choices and equipped to do well in their chosen endeavors, whatever those may be. For me and many others, Project Based Learning is the vehicle to get learners to this place of opportunity.

Win Story

Years into PBL, we now have many more stories like Skyler's—success stories of learners from high, middle, and low socioeconomic situations; success stories in rural, suburban, and urban schools; and success stories from learners who are new to speaking English. We have so many success stories at this point that I share one or two in every chapter of this book.

As I share these win stories, think about a past learner who you would have liked to have had a similar win with. Your learner's success is the heart of your "why." Let this book not only be a "how-to" for PBL but also let the stories, quotes, and possibilities inspire you toward the future you hope to offer your learners.

Fail Story

As with any change you make in your classroom, there will be areas for growth (also known as failures). It's important to anticipate that your PBL journey will not be all roses and palm trees. There will be times of risk, authenticity, and failure. But as long as you continue on your PBL journey, it's the good kind of failure—the growth mindset kind of failure we hope our learners will experience to be successful after they leave our classroom.

By modeling a healthy process for growth without requiring perfection, we teach our learners growth mindset. Modeling growth mindset, perseverance, and grit is infinitely more powerful than any worksheet, video, or book on the subject.

Despite the value of your gathering your own list of personal failures, I've included a fail story or two with each chapter to help you avoid a few common failures and learn from others' mistakes. By avoiding these failures, or at least recognizing you are not alone in them, you will be light years further than if you embarked on this journey alone. Know that this change process is never perfect, and you are in good company.

 "Perfection is the mother of procrastination."
~ Michael Hyatt

Where to Start

While all excellent journeys begin with a single step, it does require you to take a step—an action, a beginning. A ship with a working rudder can steer the captain in any direction to nearly any destination . . . unless the ship is not moving. If the ship is not moving, the rudder can go back and forth, but it will only splash the water and cause the boat to rock back and forth. Once the boat is moving, then it can move toward its destination, and the rudder can correct its course.

By picking up this book, you have started your PBL journey. You are on your way to a destination of engagement, fulfillment, and fully living out your "why." You are a brave captain with a moving ship, so you can follow the map (this book) and correct your course as you continue.

Just like your learners come from all different backgrounds, you come to this book with many experiences from different levels of understanding. Some readers may need the chapter on community partners, while others need the chapter on grading. Within each chapter, there is a description of the place to start. Whether you are a veteran to PBL or just getting started, you can find a place to start—or continue—your PBL journey.

"A journey of a thousand miles begins with a single step."
~ Chinese Proverb

Resources

In the early days of Project Based Learning, we would gather formally or informally to share resources that were working for us. For example, Steve would say, "My groups have not been awesome. Does anyone have something that helps?" and then Kate would say, "I've been using this group contract form, which has helped a ton! Want to try it out?"

We would share and create resources to solve problems or create more awesomeness. You, brave reader, have the advantage of picking up this book at a time when those resources have been created and revised over years and years of implementation with learners. At the end of every chapter, you will find relevant resources—resources to add structure and create an engaged, productive learning environment. To access these resources after each chapter, visit: https://www.magnifylearningin.org/pbl-simplified-book-resources.

Here are a few resources to get you started:

- What is PBL?
- *Finish* or *Soundtracks* by Jon Acuff (If you suffer from perfectionism, these books are the cure.)
- Where is Skyler now?
- *Start with Why—How Great Leaders Inspire Action* by Simon Sinek

Questions

Questions get us thinking about new possibilities and help us stay engaged. They work for the classroom, and I use them for this book as well. As you know, fellow educator, taking the time to write out your answers will help you solidify this work in your mind. As an additional step, you can share your answers with a friend and/or colleague. Each chapter will have questions to help you apply and get excited about this work.

- Who is your Skyler? A past learner who made a big successful turnaround? Use their name when you share. Think back through your time with them and pull out some specific details to help the memory of the experience to become more real for you.
- What are *you* hoping to gain from Project Based Learning?
- What are you hoping *your learners* will gain from Project Based Learning?

CHAPTER 1

It's Working, and It's Spreading

"The aim of education is not knowledge but action."
~ Herbert Spencer

I nevitably when you hear about Project Based Learning, some-one will say, "I have been doing Project Based Learning for years. We just didn't call it that." I propose that the PBL in this book is different than the traditional projects you might have done in class. Authenticity and community partners are a big part of that difference, but there is also a structural difference in the flow of learning, which is key to the success of your efforts. Many of the same resources you have passionately been using for years will still apply to PBL; the order just needs to change to build inquiry and empowerment. A traditional project launches after the learning has taken place, but in PBL, we want to launch the project idea and problem together right at the beginning.

Let me give you a real-world example before I launch into the process. You'll feel the difference in the order. You may be a bit uncomfortable, but uncomfortable is good. Most of the deepest learning takes place just outside of our comfort zone.

We all have great projects that involve getting out in the community. When kids get their hands dirty and make an impact, good things happen, but see if you can feel where this Project Based Learning unit changes the dynamic of even the classroom to empower learners.

When I worked with Mrs. Wisdom's third-grade class, we started with an Entry Event to launch and address two of her class's most difficult subjects: perimeter and persuasive writing. All the third-grade classes gathered in one room for the Entry Event, and instead of starting by telling this young group about standards in kid-friendly language, we inspired them with a worthy problem to solve. We brought in the executive director of the local senior center. Many of the learners have never had access to a person in charge of a social service organization, so the meeting alone broadens their horizons. The executive director talked about how senior citizens are not getting proper nutrition at home, so the lunch at the senior center is where they get the bulk of their healthy diet. The executive director explained, "The Grandpas and Grandmas in our community need help staying healthy. Would you young philanthropists like to help out?"

The third graders all enthusiastically responded that they would help. Cheers ensued as they realized they were going to be helping others; their work was going to matter. The next portion of the Entry Event involved me asking the third graders if they wanted to help the center by building raised garden beds. More cheers ensued.

I then asked if anyone knew how we could figure out how far around a garden bed it would be so that we could buy cinder blocks. After some mumbles, I finally heard someone sheepishly ask, "Perimeter?" in a tone only used in classrooms.

"Yes!" I exclaimed. "Perimeter! Who here knows how to use perimeter so well they can help us build raised garden beds?"

Now, I spent my classroom time in an eighth-grade classroom, so I didn't know that when a guest asks a question in a third-grade classroom, every hand in the room goes up. Every hand went up, and their teachers chuckled at me, shaking their heads to indicate that very few of them actually knew perimeter since it hadn't been taught yet. I rephrased my question to: "How many of you would not miss any answers on a quiz about perimeter?"

Most of the hands went down. I said, "Friends, this is not good. Do you want to help the senior citizens at the center?" More cheers. I continued, "How will we help the senior citizens improve their health if we don't know perimeter?"

Dramatic pause.

"Is there anyone in the room who can teach us perimeter?"

Dramatic pause number two.

"Mrs. Wisdom, could you teach us perimeter?"

She jumped in, "Yes! In fact, I have been teaching perimeter for ten years now."

I asked, "Young philanthropists, how many of you want to have Mrs. Wisdom teach you perimeter so that we can help the senior citizens at the center?" Cheers.

That's right! Cheers for their teacher teaching them a new standard. Maybe you get the same reaction whenever you launch your perimeter unit, but I suspect it's more likely that you just witnessed the shift in learner engagement. The PBL shift happens when learners ask to be taught standards-based subjects. **By starting with the "why" of perimeter, we engaged a room full of philanthropists excited to learn perimeter.** Please read the last sentence again carefully, so you don't miss the shift. The sentence does not say to start with perimeter; it says start with the "why" for perimeter. Perimeter has many applications in life, but the only application a learner cares about is the one that is right in front of them. The "why" for perimeter right in front of these third-grade learners is to help people just like their grandmas and grandpas to lead healthier lives. Do you need perimeter to do well in geometry your sophomore year of high school? Of course, but third graders don't care about that application yet. They only care about the "why" for learning perimeter that is closest to them. Project Based Learning brings the "why" of your standards closer to your learners, so they actually care about those standards.

Mrs. Wisdom went on to teach the same perimeter unit she taught for years, but she also taught them what a philanthropist is! She still needs best practices as she gathers and uses data to personalize the learning through workshops, but the "why" ran through the entire unit and continued to drive the project. PBL is not replacing your years of education study; it is going to reorder things and give you a new structure. And for learners, it's going to bring the "why" right up front where they can see it.

Win Story #1

Win Story #1 comes from Ellis Oliver, a quick-witted, deep-thinking sophomore at Babcock Neighborhood School in Babcock Ranch, Florida, which uses Project Based Learning as an instructional model. Ellis provides insight into Project Based Learning from a learner's perspective.

Project Based Learning is a fantastic way to engage students in learning; it allows us, students, to be hands-on with our academics. We take real-world problems, synthesize them with our classwork to find a solution, then decide on ways to culminate our ideas. I have been doing PBL for five years at Babcock Neighborhood School. The rigor and expectations can be overwhelming in the beginning, but the benefits of this learning style far outweigh memorization in traditional schools. We are in control of how we learn and convey information, which requires a great deal of out-of-the-box thinking and creativity. It is also imperative we find the strengths of each of our classmates. The beauty is that PBLs require a large variety of jobs, tasks, and opportunities, allowing every student to find their perfect fit. Sometimes you may have to step out of your comfort zone, but one guarantee is students will gain skills that will prepare them for life.

A favorite PBL was being commissioned with the job of building "Sustainable Homes," a large market in the area of our school. We researched how to make a home for the Babcock Community using solar power as well as determined appropriate materials to properly regulate the temperature in the homes. We not only had to build a 3D model of our home but placed it through temperature tests to determine efficiency. For all of these projects, we bring in community partners to help us get a better understanding of the task at hand. In this project, we invited Dr. Jennifer Languell (engineer for BNS) to present different ways to insulate our model homes. Community Partners help bring life to these projects, as well as offer opportunities to learn skills necessary in jobs. To culminate this project, we were to market and "sell" our homes.

PBL is not always fun and easy. Sometimes, we have to accept that our ideas won't work, which can be difficult. Every PBL we do is not going to be a success, just like in real life not every idea will be the right solution. It takes immense trial and error and learning from previous mistakes. If one idea is a failure, you have to move on to the next one 'till you find the perfect answer. Perseverance becomes a motto.

In standard public schools, you are learning material deemed necessary to pass the end of the course tests. In a Project Based Learning environment, we are diving deeper into the why behind our learning. Application of knowledge becomes paramount, and in turn our employability skills skyrocket. If you want to engage your learners in fun and meaningful work, I encourage you to be a part of this amazing learning style. PBL is setting me apart from other students, preparing me for future obstacles, and helping me achieve my goals as a lifelong learner. PBL ROCKS!

Win Story #2

Anne is a veteran teacher in Missouri. She has passionately taught elementary learners for fifteen years. After Anne visited a PBL Demonstration Site in Columbus, Indiana, she started her Project Based Learning journey. Anne and a small group of teachers went home and brought authentic learning experiences to their learners. The engagement from their learners was immediate! Anne exclaimed, "Why haven't I been teaching like this my whole career?"

"Never doubt that a small group of thoughtful, committed citizens can change the world; indeed, it's the only thing that ever has."
~ Margaret Mead

Anne's world has been changed by Project Based Learning, along with her learners'. We often hear how a teacher finds new life in their calling after implementing PBL.

Fail Story

Don's story is similar to Anne's story. Don has been teaching for fifteen years. It's getting more difficult for Don to stay as engaged in his classroom. The demands of testing, politics, and sixteen different initiatives on his plate are taking the joy and love out of teaching. He can't believe it, but he has thought about leaving teaching altogether. It's either that or skate along until retirement, but that's not why he got into teaching. Don got into teaching to help his learners see new opportunities they may not have seen before. He loves to see the light-bulb moments when you can visibly see learners get something! Don saw Project Based Learning come up as a training at his school, but he passed, thinking it would just be the seventeenth initiative. Besides, it seems too hard to learn something new at this point. Would he even be good at it?

Don's story is technically fictional because I don't have permission to publish any of the hundreds of stories like Don's. I hear these stories often as I travel the country talking to educators—stories of educators who know there needs to be a change, but they are unsure of the future, too afraid to change, or too worried about being perfect, so they don't change. They stay stuck in the same spot. What they are doing day in and day out will be considered good work, but they know there is something better. They got into teaching to passionately fulfill a purpose.

You are on track to living out Anne's story and skipping Don's story. I lead a national organization called Magnify Learning, which has been training passionate educators just like you for the last decade. The lessons in this book will share wins from teachers just like you who have chosen the path less traveled. They have had some fails, but they are living their "why," and that has made all the difference. The PBL journey is worth it for you and the learners you love.

Bottom Line: Wherever you are in your education journey, you can start using Project Based Learning and witness the transformation firsthand.

Where to Start

In the early days of Project Based Learning, starting meant a ton of trial and error with long nights spent trying to create structures and processes to help learners know their new, engaged role. Today, with the advancements, workshops, and resources in Project Based Learning, you can get started in a number of ways with a plethora of available resources.

I recommend you start by visiting a school that is currently engaging in Project Based Learning. If you ask around a bit, you can likely find a school where people say there is Project Based Learning happening. At Magnify Learning, we have Demonstration Sites you can visit. We can send you to Columbus, IN, Indianapolis, IN, Neosho, MO, or Babcock Ranch, Florida and guarantee that you will see high-quality Project Based Learning in action. As a side note, Babcock Ranch Neighborhood School is the closest site to the best beach of any of the areas listed above!

Resources

All resources listed can be found at: www.magnifylearningin.org/pbl-simplified-book-resources.

- *PBL Simplified* Podcast
  - You can hear from teachers in the classroom just like you and get leadership lessons for sustaining your PBL work.
- *PBL Simplified* Video Series

- Three- to five-minute videos on key PBL topics
- What is PBL?
- Demonstration Sites

Questions

- What do you like about the story of Mrs. Wisdom?
- What do you wonder about the story of Mrs. Wisdom?
- What are your key motivations for starting your PBL journey?
- Who can you ask to join you on your PBL journey?

CHAPTER 2

Step 1: Define the Problem

*"Your ability to solve problems and make good
decisions is the true measure of your skill as a leader."*
~ Brian Tracy

To help you feel the flow of a PBL project, the next six chapters are in the order of the six steps within a PBL Unit. The key to finishing a project well is starting a project well. Before launching a PBL Unit, we identify the standards and the real-world problem our learners will be solving. We then launch our unit with an Entry Event that is meant to build enthusiasm for the work and lay out the desired outcomes.

In planning a PBL, we start with the standards we are going to engage partly because we live in a world engrossed in standardized testing, but also because the standards are the basis of the content we want our learners to engage. If we are addressing a real-world problem, we are going to run into standards left and right. In the real world, people are reading and writing nonfiction texts, creating budgets, figuring perimeter, performing experiments, and so on.

"Persistence and resilience only come from having been given the chance to work through difficult problems."
~ Gever Tulley

Find the meaty standards with the most practical application, whatever it is you call them—power standards, critical standards, etc. Basically, choose argumentative writing over haikus. Argumentative writing is a power standard affecting many critical thinking skills from defending a position with evidence to writing for an audience. Argumentative writing is a power standard because it helps learners in multiple ways and builds useful skills they will use beyond school. Haikus are also a standard for poetry, but a learner is unlikely to need them beyond school, and the content is unlikely to help in other areas. For each PBL Unit, you might be spending four weeks on it, so make sure the standards you include are worthy of that time.

Choosing your standards is like making your financial budget. When your money is gone, you can't buy anything else, so you must make sure you are buying the things you really need. When your year is over, you don't get to teach more, so use your time well by diving deep into meaningful standards. Argumentative writing is like buying your main dinner items, and haikus is like buying cotton candy. It is not possible to teach all your standards fully in a given year, so make sure you are choosing your PBL standards with intentionality. A PBL Unit often gives teachers more flexibility and applies to more standards than a traditional unit, so you may find that you can address more than one standard in a PBL single unit. For instance, those speaking and listening skills you gloss over each year will fit into any PBL Unit in which you are presenting to an outside audience, so include those along with your argumentative writing standards.

Once you know the set of standards you are going to engage, you can launch your Entry Event to define the problem. To ensure the authenticity of your problem, plan to have a community partner come in to launch the Entry Event. If your problem is a real-world problem, there should be real people in the real world working on this real problem. These people will want to come in and talk to your learners because most people want to help and are passionate about their work. We will cover community partners in depth in Chapter 8. For now, know that you need a real-world problem your learners can participate in through learning the standards. To frame the problem throughout the project, you must first develop a driving question.

Your driving question will be a single overarching question for your entire PBL Unit. It's like an umbrella under which all aspects of your unit will take place, so it needs to be open-ended, have multiple solutions, and, at the very least, be non-Googleable. If I can Google the answer or answer with a "yes" or "no," the question is not deep enough to investigate for four weeks. A close-ended question with known solutions also doesn't get your learners thinking critically about innovative solutions.

The driving question will be a home base for your PBL. As you complete workshops and work through the other steps of PBL, you will continue to reference that driving question. The driving question should be at the front of the room throughout the entire PBL Unit, and your learners should be able to recite it to me if I were to visit your classroom. Some PBL teachers keep all their driving questions posted on their walls for the whole year, so you can quickly see all the authentic work the learners are engaged in.

As an example, if you are in the heart of a genetics PBL in Step 3, talking about Punnett Squares, you can reference back to your driving question to remind learners of the why: "How can we as young scientists help educate families about genetic diseases when their children are first diagnosed so they are better prepared to face the effects?" The driving question reminds your learners of the impact they are making in the world. This "noble why" guides the deep content learning and brings about empowerment and engagement when learners are no longer learning content just to pass a test.

"Every project is an opportunity to learn, to figure out problems and challenges, to invent and reinvent."
~ David Rockwell

At-Risk Driving Questions	Proficient Driving Questions
Why do we need slope intercept formula?	How can we as economists help people understand the relationship between supply and demand so that they can create the best business possible?
What are the causes of the Civil War?	How do we as political advisors educate our community on how a divided country negatively or positively affects the future success of a nation so that citizens can take positive action?

Why is exercise important?	How do we as fitness experts create a customized training plan for busy professionals so they can achieve their best life?
What are some ways perimeter is important?	How can our third-grade nutritionists help provide better food options to the senior center so that senior citizens have an improved quality of life?

To develop a benchmark for Step 1, have your learners develop Problem Statements and Driving Questions. Have learners first identify their understanding of the problem being presented. If we're looking at the genetics Driving Question, a possible Problem Statement could be: Families who have children with genetic diseases could use help learning more about the disease and how to best care for their children.

Then have learners restate the driving question in their own words to show they understand their role and assignment. To complement our teacher-created Driving Question, a student Driving Question might state: How do I as a genetics specialist create a public service announcement to educate parents about the genetic disease of their child so they can be more prepared to care for their child's unique needs?

The generic format of a Driving Question follows:

How can we as a _____ (role),

do/create _____ (action verb with end product)

so that _____ (what happens because of the work)?

Learners should present a well-thought-out Driving Question before moving on to Step 2. Embedded in the PBL process is an opportunity for learners to see themselves in roles that may be new to them. Learners are now writing, creating, and presenting from the seat of an author, marketer, scientist, educator, museum curator, or whatever role you have for them. Role identity has a significant impact on how learners see themselves in the future.[1]

Your Entry Event will build excitement, invite inquiry, and inspire engagement around your PBL Unit. Doesn't that sound like a great way to start a unit? Step 2 will then communicate your expectations to learners *after* they understand the "why" and their role in solving the problem.

Win Story

The director of the Benjamin Harrison Home came into our class to launch an Entry Event. He had a real-world problem. The Benjamin Harrison Home went out to schools to perform workshops. The elementary school workshops were requested often, but the middle school courses were rarely requested. The director charged our learners with the task of creating the next generation of programming for the Benjamin Harrison Home. During the Entry Event, learners experienced the original middle school programming knowing they would be the ones creating a new program for schools across the state to purchase. What a real-world problem to solve! Eighth-grade learners wrote programming for a real nonprofit organization for real-life schools to buy and run with learners. There were some stipulations, which is a nice lead-in to Step 2. The Benjamin Harrison Home stipulated a budget of $500, the presentation could not use Wi-Fi, and the presentation needed to address content standards for middle schoolers. The goal was to engage the content of the Benjamin Harrison Home and make it exciting for middle school learners. The authentic audience was the Benjamin Harrison Home, which would select the best programming to implement. This was a powerful "why" that allowed the students to make a difference beyond the walls of a classroom.

Win Story #2

This win story comes from veteran PBL educator, Andrew Larson. Andrew is a facilitator of learning at CSA New Tech in Columbus, IN. Read on to learn about the authenticity of the research involved in this PBL Unit as his learners jumped in and discovered a yeast that was not classified in North America by any scientist—ever!

In terms of wins, the biggest came in my AP Biology class in 2013– 2014. A conversation with an old friend and lab mate from Purdue named John Cavaletto led to a partnership. He would make the two-hour drive to Columbus (twice) in order to have my learners participate in a research project he was running. The project was a biodiversity survey of phylloplane yeast, ubiquitous species found on almost every plant surface. Our job was to gather them, culture the yeast in Petri dishes, and purify the colonies.

Next, John facilitated the preparation of samples for Polymerase Chain Reaction (PCR), the same procedure used to detect coronavirus in COVID-19 tests. He ran the PCR at school in a toaster-sized thermocycler and then took the samples back to Purdue for DNA sequencing. When the results were in, he sent links back to us that revealed matches to samples in a global database for our analysis. A pure culture of phylloplane yeast is distinct in appearance; they aren't fuzzy like the mold you'd find on old bread but are instead slimy (more like bacteria.) And the one that we isolated was day-glow pink. And to think that it was isolated from the leaf of a Japanese Yew in someone's neighborhood in the dead of winter . . . science is amazing!

The results revealed that one of the samples collected by our learners had never before been characterized in North America. While this discovery has not yet led to a cure for cancer, it contributed to the body of scientific information, and that is the holy grail for all science teachers, as far as I can tell. The project went on to be awarded the Best-In-Network Prize for Authenticity in the New Tech Network in 2014. In addition to that recognition, we were required to produce a video highlighting the project, which my learners created, and which was played for a full ballroom of educators at the national conference. Our local newspaper ran the story, as did the Purdue Alumni Association. It was a special time.

When we first received the news and the links from John that revealed the rarity of our discovery, my learners didn't seem to believe it. Maybe it seemed like a sweepstakes mailer. For sure, in order to believe it, they needed to undergo a shift in thinking because science has typically been presented as a body of knowledge to master and not a process of discovery. What makes this project a huge win in my book is that it presents science as an enterprise in which the public is welcome to endeavor. That's the ah-ha that my learners had.

Another important takeaway from this project is that, as educators, we don't have to have all of the ideas and create all of the magic from scratch. In this case all that happened was that I welcomed my friend into our classroom in the same way that he welcomed us into his research. It was synergistic. I think that a lot of great projects can create great opportunities for learners when we slide into some existing framework; maybe it's an essay contest, or an entrepreneurial challenge being offered up by the local chamber of commerce. It's not cheating. It's being resourceful.

It is also important to point out that even if we hadn't lucked into a scientific discovery, this project is still a win (I've repeated it at least two times and we had no further firsts in the sense of the yeast species and the prize). You've heard the old adage that one "creates their own luck," and I believe that in this case, that's what happened. We got lucky because we took a chance on the project.

Fail Story

I decided to take on world hunger with my learners. I presented the real-world problem to them and waited for the magic to happen. It turns out all my learners thought all hungry people were in Africa and that the primary solution to this problem would be canned goods. I wanted to protect their voice, so I ran with it. I asked them how they would afford the shipping costs, and they wanted to have a car wash. I asked them how they would provide the materials for a car wash, so they sold suckers at lunch. And on . . . and on . . . it grew! Soon we were selling suckers to wash cars, so we could raise nearly $5,000 to send canned goods to people we didn't know. The learners were passionate and excited, but the excitement began to wane as time went on.

Eventually I stopped the madness and suggested we try to help out the local food pantry, at which point, one learner mentioned his mom volunteered there and could take anything we wanted to the community center for free.

Wait, what? How did we miss that?

Sanity triumphed, and we made a difference in our part of the world with the influence we had at the time. From this failure, I've learned to think globally but act locally. I never would have learned this lesson if I hadn't been willing to try and fail. My learners learned right along with me. I was transparent with this fail, and we were all able to evaluate and internalize the process of helping others. Several local community service initiatives and a nonprofit were birthed out of that class, and all were initiated from the learners, not me. They learned the process because I allowed my failure to be public and my learning to be transparent.

**Bottom Line: Authentic Project Based Learning has
its foundations in standards and a real-world problem.**

Where to Start

Start by digging into your standards and developing your power standards. Not all standards are created equal. As I mentioned earlier, haikus are a standard just like argumentative writing is a standard. One of these two is more likely to help your learners problem-solve, back up their answers with reason, and perform well on standardized tests. Hopefully you know which one by now, but either way, you should engage in the conversation. Developing power standards is not a new idea. The discussion has already started, so do some research and see what others are prioritizing. Twitter or Google are pretty good places to engage in this conversation at the time of this writing.

Once you identify some power standards, you have an excellent place to start a PBL Unit. Immerse your project in authenticity and standards. It is hard to find an authentic problem that doesn't relate to standards, and knowing which standards are going to most empower your learners for the future is a reliable place to start.

Resources

All resources listed can be found at:
www.magnifylearningin.org/pbl-simplified-book-resources.

- PBL Planning Forms
- Driving Questions
  - Templates and guiding slide deck
- *PBL Simplified* Podcast
  - PBL Showcase Episodes share PBL Unit ideas from facilitators from around the country
  - PBL Leadership episodes support leaders with sustainable implementation of PBL

Questions

- What's a problem your learners can solve?
- What community partner could be involved with this project?
- Who can you share your PBL Unit idea with to get quick feedback?

CHAPTER 3

Step 2: Solution Criteria

"People fail forward toward success."
~ Mary Kay Ash

With Step 1 complete, you have launched an authentic, standards-based problem, and your learners are excited to engage in a solution. Step 2 is the process of adding structure to the problem to ensure you lead learners down a successful path. The popular mantra has been: "We need to make space for kids to fail." There is some truth in that statement; our learners need a place where they are empowered to do the work well, and it's even more exciting to see our learners succeed after they have struggled. But it's also our job to set up the environment for the best chance of success.

On the practical side, I include establishing rubrics and limits related to the project as part of this chapter, which will drive our Need to Knows. In Step 1, learners are dreaming of solutions to a problem. They may be dreaming of camel rides, hot air balloons, and satellites dropping food for those in need. Dreaming is a crucial component to success and inquiry, but our learners have likely never really engaged in real-world problems and don't understand the liability, permits, and cost involved with bringing their ideas to fruition. Our job in Step 2 is to add appropriate structure, along with encouragement, to ensure success. Structure does not have to kill creativity.

 "In limits, there is freedom. Creativity thrives within structure."
~ Julia Cameron

While research backs up the benefits of structure, the allegory of the school for the blind illustrates it best. There were once facilitators at an elementary school for blind learners who were trying to help maximize recess time. The learners had two acres of playground to play on, but the learners would step out the door and only go about twenty yards. They could hear the cars on the far side of the two-acre playground and would stay close to the door despite the consistent assurance of their trusted facilitators that they had plenty of room to go out and play. A new facilitator joined the staff who understood the importance of structure as a safety net to bring more creativity, and she suggested a fence on the outskirts of the playground. With the fence installed along the road at the far edge of the playground, the learners cautiously walked out toward the new fence. With the guidance and encouragement of their facilitators, the learners went out and touched the fence and heard the cars. They ran and cartwheeled back toward the school with some occasional somersaults. From that day forward, the learners knew the fence was there and the space in between was for them. They could now explore the playground on their own knowing the structure would keep them on the right track. Structure is good for our learners and for us.

One important piece of structure is a rubric. Rubrics should be presented to learners early in a project, so they know what the expectations are. We also present rubrics early so that we can generate inquiry. As learners look through the rubric, they encounter ideas they have not learned about and will have questions. These questions will come out as Need to Knows and will help drive sustained inquiry throughout your project. For instance, when a learner encounters the word angioplasty on your rubric, they are going to need that defined to achieve their project goal. We let them ask the question, "What is angioplasty?" and we say, "Great question! Thank you for asking that. We are going to need to have mastery of these terms to solve this problem. Would you like me to schedule a workshop to help answer your question?"

What you do through that process is validate their question, provide reassurance that you will answer future questions, and open the door for you to teach a workshop on one of your standards. Need to Knows will continue to build as learners explore the rubric:

- "When is this due?"
- "Do we get to work in groups?"
- "What technology can we use to present?"
- "What is a compound-complex sentence?"
- "How do we talk with a doctor?"

Need to Knows vary in importance, so it is helpful to organize them into categories for yourself and learners. Find categories that work for you, but always separate a logistical Need to Know such as "When do we present?" from a content-driven Need to Know like "What is angioplasty?". The Need to Knows document should be a living document to help sustain inquiry throughout the project. As the project begins, you will start to answer Need to Knows through workshops, and together, you and your learners will move ideas over to a Know column. The constant movement from Need to Know to Know will show everyone that learning is taking place and that learning is ongoing. As learners develop more knowledge about a topic, more focused Need to Knows will arise, which is another great experience. Validating each new Need to Know builds a culture of inquiry.

A culture of inquiry is a powerful force working in the background of your classroom. Textbooks may label a "bell ringer question" or "attention getter" as the inquiry of a unit, but those are very surface-level inquiries. You want a culture of inquiry where learners are curious and they know you will validate their questions and answer them. As you build a culture of inquiry, it becomes a current that moves your learners along. A new learner or community partner will feel that current and be moved along by it. Questions and curiosity become the norm, and you no longer have to force them on learners. With inquiry and wonder, learner engagement is happening through the culture, not just your actions.

One question I often get from teachers who are new to having their learners ask questions is: "What do I do if my core standards do not come up within my first Need to Know session?" I tell them there is an art to Need to Knows. We want our learners to be empowered to drive their learning, so we want them to ask questions that will lead to scheduled workshops. We also want to lead learners to new heights they would not achieve on their own, so they will need some guidance until they develop a culture of inquiry. The quick answer to the question above is that you still need to teach your standards, so you need to make sure they come up in that first Need to Know session. Here are a few example questions to help you develop inquiry and spark more questions from your learners:

- "Did anybody notice in the middle of the rubric where it talks about Punnett Squares? Do we know what Punnett Squares are?"
- "How many of you have ever written a letter to a local government official? Would a workshop on writing a letter be helpful?"
- "I know you have studied Western cultures before, but would anyone like a refresher workshop?"
- "Did you notice we are using at least two new technologies? Does anyone want a workshop about the different possibilities we have?"

Any of those questions is more empowering than a list of things we must do because the state says so. Once you have a Need to Know on the board, you have license to teach it, so make sure your core standards are on the list. If you haven't perfected this art form yet, you may need to say something more direct like: "Hey everyone, the writing process didn't come up, but I need to hold a workshop on the writing process, so you can produce the best possible letter to your local government official. I'm going to put it up here. Is that okay?" In the context of Need to Knows, adding workshops this way is still better than: "You have to learn this because I said so."

"One of the fastest ways to find the solution to an issue or challenge you are facing is to ask the right questions."
~ Robin S. Sharma

Data-driven Need to Knows is another way to make sure you are holding workshops your learners need even if they do not ask. If you ask a room full of eighth graders if they know compound sentences, the majority of them will say, "Of course! We did those in sixth grade!" But what each learner is really saying is a bit different from the next learner, and it's not because they are being difficult or misleading. Every learner has their own unique take. For example:

- When Billy says, "Of course!" he really means, "I remember Mrs. Smith talking about those."
- When Adele says, "Of course!" she really means, "I can point out a compound sentence, but I can't make my own."
- When Yozabeth says, "Of course!" she really means, "I can spot them, and I put a comma in there every other time, so I'm right half the time."
- When Jay says, "Of course!" he means, "I can join two independent clauses with a conjunction and a comma."

None of these learners is trying to be deceptive. They just have different ways of seeing school. A well-crafted, twenty-question pre-test on sentence types can create defined groups with different instructional needs. These data-driven Need to Knows cannot be argued because the data can show whether a learner has this Need to Know or not. Learners do not get to choose these workshops.

Each of these learners would attend a different workshop with some of them likely testing out.

Ultimately, the Need to Knows you establish give you significant leverage for the inevitable education question, "Why are we doing this?" With a solid Need to Know process, you can truthfully answer, "We are running this workshop because you asked me to. Remember, this workshop is based on this Need to Know and will help enhance your solution and presentation." Again, this is a much better answer than our typical answers of "Because the state says we should" or "Because you will need it in college". Those "whys" might be true, but they are too far away from the learners. We want to present the "why" that is closest to the learner since this is the one they will have the most engagement with.

Did you feel the switch again? Learners are now asking you to teach!

In one day, you have launched an engaging project and set up a structure to help guide your learners to a successful outcome. You have framed your standards in the real world with a "why" that is larger than a grade. Now the learners are pushing instead of you pulling them along. Only once the problem is identified and structured are we ready to start looking at possible solutions.

Win Story #1

Developing success criteria with learners can be a big win because we make sure learners are headed in the right direction. When I move rubrics up to the front of the PBL process, I find learners are much more likely to be on the right track. All my learners turned in the first three projects I assigned as a PBL teacher. This completion rate was monumental considering I was used to the typical 20 percent or so of learners who just wouldn't bother. This success actually led to more grading on my part because everyone turned things in, but it was a good problem to have. I attribute much of that success to the clarity learners had from day one of the PBL. Right out of the gate, learners knew the expectations, and if they had questions, they had ample opportunity to ask and were encouraged to do so.

Win Story #2

I had the learner with the lowest formative assessment score in the school, which meant that out of 951 learners, Simon had the lowest score for this online exam. Certainly he didn't try, but he also had some recognized learning issues. With a Project Based Learning process, we saw his scores skyrocket. The first twenty-five-point gain was because he was trying for the first time in a while. This shows how PBL can redirect apathy. He then saw even more continued improvement that brought him very close to grade level. This second continuous gain was because he began to ask questions again. He was used to asking questions and being too far behind for anyone to have time to help him. With the Need to Know process, he saw his questions turned into workshops, usually with other learners who had the same questions. Some workshops he even tested out of, which was new for him too. He was accustomed to being part of the group that the special education teacher came and got during work time, whether he needed help or not. By differentiating the workshops for Simon's needs and showing him that his questions were being answered, he reengaged and asked more questions, which led to more learning.

Fail Story

In one Need to Know session, I stopped to answer a Need to Know because I thought it would add clarity. It was a good intention, but instead what happened is that I ended up skewing all of the other Need to Knows. I stopped to talk about one of the new technologies we would be using in the project, and suddenly we ended up with a whole list of technological Need to Knows, which were not part of the power standards I was trying to lead learners to with this PBL. This class asked more technology questions and less standards-based questions. To fix the problem, I took the Need to Knows from my other class periods and melded them together to create a more complete list that still authentically came from my learners. It takes practice, discipline, and trust to give learners some control over their learning, and sometimes we need to stay out of the way. If we want to have learners actively participate in their education, we have to give them a voice.

Bottom Line: Success Criteria will show learners where the goal is and the parameters they must work within.

Where to Start

Ask your learners what they already know about a topic and what they need to know to become more advanced in a subject. Give a quick pre-test to see what learners already know about your unit. Then ask where they are curious. Asking learners questions about what they want to learn is empowering. They will likely guide you in the direction you have already planned, but they want to have the voice to say they wanted to go that way. Take just fifteen minutes and try it out.

Resources

All resources listed can be found at
https://www.magnifylearningin.org/pbl-simplified-book-resources

- Know/Need to Know
- Rubrics and Assessments
  - PBL Rubric Examples

Questions

- Will giving up some control in your classroom be an area of growth for you?
- Have you witnessed a time when structure allowed learners to actually have *more* freedom?
- How can you use your rubrics to help communicate expectations as well as give a grade?
- What do you envision an advanced end product will look like?

CHAPTER 4

Step 3: Solution Research

"Research is formalized curiosity.
It is poking and prying with a purpose."
~ Zora Neale Hurston

"Why does the kid who didn't do any work get the same grade as my child?"

"I'll just do all the work because then I know it will be right."

"Well, they just did the work, so I let them."

These familiar statements make everyone dread group work. That's why we leverage Step 3 to diffuse these often-valid comments by keeping learners working individually until Step 4.

Group work is important for teaching learners about collaboration, but it isn't the only way to teach collaboration. You can use protocols that help learners work together even if they are not in formal groups yet. After all, if collaboration is all about getting learners in groups, then the lunchroom would take care of all our collaboration needs. But we know the lunchroom does not help with meaningful collaboration. It lacks the structures, purpose, and meaning for any type of useful collaboration. I talk about creating meaningful groups in the next chapter and show you how to set up a solid group contract to provide the structure your groups need to be less awful, but in Step 3, Solution Research, you are guiding your learners through the bulk of their standards-based content work.

Step 3 is when you are benchmarking learning, immersed in the full context of the project. You are making sure your learners are mastering their standards through content workshops that are created based on learner Need to Knows and data-driven Need to Knows from Step 2. Note that you should be taking grades in these workshops to prove learning. By recording the learning and taking grades in Step 3, you can create a more authentic presentation time. Your learners can use their presentation time to display their innovative solution to the real-world problem instead of reciting facts so that you can record their grade.

 "Tell me and I forget. Teach me and I remember. Involve me and I learn."
~ Benjamin Franklin

Need to Know Workshops

In Step 1, you launched your PBL Unit and created excitement, engagement, and curiosity. In Step 2, you asked your learners what they Need to Know in order to achieve a solution to the real-world problem. Step 2 creates a list of workshops your learners asked for. In Step 3, you are taking those Need to Knows and turning them into workshops. In many cases, these workshops are centered around the best-practice teaching you have been doing for years.

If you are engaging your learners in a perimeter workshop like Mrs. Wisdom did in Chapter 1, you will begin by pointing out that the learners asked for this workshop. Remember, this is the secret sauce. You have learners asking you to teach them, so they can best achieve their solution to the real-world problem. Mrs. Wisdom's front board would display the main driving question, the workshop-driving question, and objectives and would look something like this:

Driving Question: How can our third-grade class help provide better nutrition to the senior center so that senior citizens have an improved quality of life?

Workshop Driving Question: How can we master perimeter to ensure we order the correct number of cinder blocks for the garden beds?

Objectives: Learners will be able to:

- Find the perimeter of a given object on a worksheet
- Measure the perimeter of a real-life object
- Plan out a scale drawing of a garden bed

Learners in this perimeter workshop know why they are learning perimeter. They can see how it relates to today's lesson and how it connects to the overall PBL Unit. Mrs. Wisdom will likely have some direct instruction on perimeter, give some examples, create practice time, and give a quiz or test to determine learner mastery.

Mrs. Wisdom also creates workshops for her learners to get caught up. If a learner received 80 percent or less on the final perimeter mastery quiz, the learner has a mandated opportunity to improve their understanding of perimeter. Mrs. Wisdom holds a catch-up workshop for these learners, so they can best create a real-world solution to the problem at hand. That sounds much better than: "We don't have time to catch you up, so try to learn it on your own." or "You have to take this remediation class because you are not good at math." We want to frame all the learning under the umbrella of the authentic Driving Question, which drives our learning together.

What are the other learners doing while Mrs. Wisdom is holding this small-group, catch-up workshop? This is the million-dollar differentiation question, and it's one of the main reasons Project Based Learning is so successful. I find PBL offers the real solution to differentiation, so you don't have to create yet another set of learning for the differentiated tracks. While Mrs. Wisdom is working in a small group with learners who need individualized attention with perimeter, the other learners are moving forward by creating their garden bed plans. They are measuring and planning what will go in the garden. PBL gives the other learners in the class meaningful work to do while Mrs. Wisdom is working with the catch-up learners on their individual needs in a ten- to fifteen-minute workshop with a check for understanding at the end. This individualization is one of the secret sauces of Project Based Learning. The individualization through workshops allows learners with Individual Education Plans (IEPs) to exceed expectations.

First, learners with IEPs have a safety net that allows them to get the just-in-time teaching they need. Second, the workshop model takes away the stigma often associated with the extra help—the situation where a special education teacher pokes her head in and says, "My five come with me." Instead, we have a situation where anyone who needs help (you know you have some learners who should be receiving services but aren't) comes to get help because getting help isn't a bad thing. Getting help is part of having a growth mindset. We all need to get help in certain areas, so we can perform at our best.

All of this will take place before the presentation. Please do not wait to grade all the content knowledge until the five-minute presentation at the conclusion of your PBL. In the vein of allowing for failure, you can certainly try and see for yourself, but there are several reasons why taking standards-based grades in Step 3 works well for you and the learner.

First, you cannot grade all the content standards of four group members presenting during a five-minute period. Imagine you have a room with four learners in the front and you are sitting with five community partners watching their five-minute presentation. Your community partners are giving feedback on paper, but they are only giving "I likes" and "I wonders" (that part is a good idea). Now imagine yourself with four rubrics in front of you with five different indices ranging from presentation skills, such as eye contact, to content skills, such as perimeter, compound sentences, important dates, and Punnett Square mastery. Then, imagine yourself doing this for all your learners! If your blood pressure went up just imagining the scenario, you got it right. You end up frazzled, and it would be very surprising if you are able to give a fair assessment of your learners' mastery.

Secondly, and most importantly, when you try grading all the content in the presentation, the presentation becomes less authentic and more school-ish. Instead of presenting their creative solution to eradicating invasive species in the local park to the Department of Natural Resources, your learners are regurgitating the same facts over and over again to make sure they get their grade. Also, your groups will all be presenting the same content information over and over again to get their grades. If you begin to notice the exact same information being presented over and over again, it is a sign that your PBL Unit is not authentic, and it is boring for the community partner. If this happens to you, don't fret; record your failure, and keep this chapter in mind as you plan your next PBL Unit.

Wouldn't it be great if the Department of Natural Resources walked away with seven to ten new ideas from your learners? Free up the presentation to be as authentic as possible. Record evidence of learning throughout Step 3 and then let the presentation in Step 5 be as authentic as possible for your professional audience.

 "Research is to see what everybody else has seen, and to think what nobody else has thought."
~ Albert Szent-Gyorgyi

You can still have your traditional benchmarks such as quizzes and tests to see if learners have mastered their standards or if they need additional helps. In fact, you want to work on mastering the standards before the presentation for two reasons. First, you want your learners to be extremely prepared to show off their newfound knowledge and expertise. Secondly, it tends to be more difficult to fill in any learning gaps after the project is over. If we tackle the learning gaps during Step 3, they are still under the umbrella of the project. We also have the added engagement to say, "We are holding this workshop to get you all caught up on this writing standard, so you are best prepared for your group work and your final presentation." As we help learners catch up, it is useful to have that additional context and motivation for them.

In Step 3, we are capitalizing on the inquiry and engagement we created with the Entry Event. Learners understand the big picture of the project, and they also understand there are things they need to learn to achieve their goal. Once we have engagement, we capitalize on it with academic rigor! When engagement goes up, we can increase the rigor. If you increase the rigor without increasing the engagement, you will have a masterfully planned lesson that nobody fully engages with. Increase the engagement level and *then* turn up the heat on the rigor.

Win Story #1

Based on the Fail Story of the teacher trying to grade all the learners' content knowledge during the presentation, I came away with two critical wins I think everyone should consider. The first is to make Steps 1–3 as individual as possible. Individualization from the start creates an environment in which everyone is accountable for their own learning. It doesn't mean learners cannot collaborate; it means learners cannot hide in a group. Individual quizzes and benchmarks allow us to know who is on track and who needs more help before the big presentation day.

Win Story #2

The second win would be to ensure that there is always a practice presentation day. We must have a practice presentation day, so we know what learners are going to say. Presentation day is game day. There is not a whole lot of instruction you can do during a presentation, so you should have a pretty good idea of what the presentations are going to be like before you get community partners in the room.

Emily presented her idea to her teacher and a small group of her peers very early on in the process to get feedback on her idea. This early, low-stress tuning presentation helped learners get used to presenting as well. Her teacher had a huge win during this early Tuning Protocol because Emily was way off in left field with her idea. The real-world problem they were solving was to create a small business with a focus on green energy. Emily presented her desire to help animals get adopted at the local animal shelter with little to no connection to the rubric or the driving question. The win was that Emily had time to rework her plan and created a wonderful presentation in time because this early presentation time revealed her error with time to correct it. Watching her present her left-field topic in front of a panel during a final presentation would have been awful for everyone involved. With time to rework, Emily presented her business idea to a panel of local business leaders with pride.

Fail Story

As I sit ready to show off the great work my learners have created to a panel of community partners, I smile. The project was authentic, it launched well, the end product is exciting, so I wait in eager anticipation. Then I hear presentation after presentation in which the most energetic academic learner talks 90 percent of the time and the others sit back, watch, and only answer questions directly sent their way. My smile fades, and I ponder. Then I ask questions:

Me: "Why didn't you talk during the presentation?"

Learner: "She knew more than me, so I just let her go."

Me: "You did research though. Why didn't you talk about that?"

Learner: "My role was to find pictures off of Google."

Me: "Oh."

Practice presentations will come up again, but let me take a moment to emphasize their importance now. This fail story could have been avoided altogether if I would have allotted time for learners to practice in front of me and their peers. You need to institute the benchmark of a practice presentation because you need to know what your learners are going to say, and your learners need a smaller stress test before presenting in front of community partners.

Bottom Line: By the end of Step 3, learners should be equipped to contribute to the group with researched solutions and content knowledge.

Where to Start

Create an engaging opportunity for learners to dive into their research. Keep all your typical benchmarks, so you know things are going in the right direction, but instead of just presenting the information in a lecture, determine which topics need to come from you and which ones your learners can discover on their own. Scaffold this process if your learners are not used to open research by giving them credible websites or apps to visit for the information. Letting untrained learners roam free on Google in hopes that they find useful information is an excellent way to catalog your own Fail Story.

Resources

All resources listed can be found at:

www.magnifylearningin.org/pbl-simplified-book-resources.

- 6 Step Process of PBL
  - Big picture overview of PBL
- Scaffolding
  - Guide to help you develop lessons, activities, and workshops
- Inquiry

Questions

- What is a Fail Story you have for group work?
- How could some of the ideas in this chapter have helped that situation?
- Can you coordinate with an English teacher to provide a workshop on research best practices?

CHAPTER 5

Step 4: Pick a Solution

*"Collaboration is like carbonation for fresh ideas.
Working together bubbles up ideas you would not
have come up with solo, which gets you further faster."*
~ Caroline Ghosn

N ow that all your learners have researched solutions for the problem and participated in content workshops, they are appropriately equipped to actively participate in a group. By holding off group work until Step 4, we create a situation in which the bulk of a learner's grade is based on their individual work. We also create a situation in which group members do not depend on each other until they are better equipped and have wrestled with the problem(s), research, and solution(s) individually. Note that while keeping things individual until Step 4 can help the process, it does not mean that learners know how to efficiently work in teams, divide work, or pick the best solution, so I include a discussion of groups in this chapter.

Before we enter the world of group structures and dynamics, I want to put it out there that it is okay to have groups of one for an entire project. The first PBL project you embark on may be a great place to try out groups of one. Groups of one will allow *you* to acclimate to the learning flow of PBL, as well as your learners. Like any good science experiment, you may not want to change too many variables at the same time. Once you and your learners are accustomed to the new vocabulary and structure, groups can be a fantastic way to equip our learners with the collaboration skills the workforce is looking for and the general interpersonal skills often lacking in our graduates. A recent survey noted, "Employers want job candidates with 'uniquely human' skills, but finding those candidates isn't easy. Nearly 3 in 4 employers say they have a hard time finding graduates with soft skills their companies need."[2]

To make sure your first foray into PBL group work is successful, it is essential to have enough structure to capture your wins and learn from your failures.

 "Unity is strength . . . when there is teamwork and collaboration, wonderful things can be achieved."
~ Mattie Stepanek

Group Contracts

Group contracts are significant structural and accountability pieces, and they add an air of professionalism to the process for learners. Critical components of the group contract are:

- Defined roles
- Strengths/weaknesses
- Contact information

- Firing clause
- Signature lines

A defined role rewards learners when their area goes well and helps us as educators diagnose a problem when a group is having trouble. Without well-defined roles, it is difficult to hold learners accountable for their work. The typical accountability conversation you have likely experienced might sound like this:

> **You:** "Your group says you aren't doing any work, Ryan."
>
> **Ryan:** "That's crazy! They won't even tell me what to do."
>
> **You:** "What have you been doing?"
>
> **Ryan:** "I've been trying to do a ton of work, but they keep doing it all before I can get started."
>
> **You:** "So . . . what have you been doing?"
>
> **Ryan:** "You know. Stuff. I've been doing stuff this whole time."

While Ryan is passionately defending himself in the conversation above, it doesn't present a solution. Defined roles in the group allows the same conversation to possibly go like this:

> **You:** "Your group says you aren't doing any work, Ryan."
>
> **Ryan:** "That's crazy! They won't even tell me what to do."

You: "What is your role according to the group contract?"

Ryan: "I'm the Rubric Guru."

You: "Great! You are perfect for that role. The group contract states the Rubric Guru will be checking each stage of the PBL to make sure that the rubric requirements are being met. Are you doing that?"

Ryan: "See! Yes, I am. We are mostly on track. Except for this section right here."

You: "How are you tracking that information?"

Ryan: (taps the side of his head) "It's all right here."

You: "It would likely help your group dynamics if you can communicate your work to the rest of the group. How can you show the rest of the group where they are with the rubric?"

Ryan: "I could highlight sections of the rubric to show what we have completed and what is still needed."

You: "Perfect! I'll look for that tomorrow."

In this case, Ryan believes he has done the work while the rest of the group sees him doing nothing. The defined roles in the group contract would allow you to hold Ryan accountable to a written group contract instead of talking in circles about emotional group dynamics. Defined roles bring clarity to groups.

By listing the strengths and weaknesses of each group member, every learner has the opportunity to self-assess and make a case for why they believe they should have a specific role or not. When you look at some of the group contracts listed in the resource section at the end of this chapter, you will see tables where learners can have a guided conversation about their strengths and weaknesses before choosing roles. You can even run a protocol to keep groups on track during this process:

- **3 minutes**: Learners individually write down their strengths and weaknesses from a given list on the board
- **30 seconds per person**: Share their strengths and how they can benefit the group
- **30 seconds per person**: Share their weaknesses and the work they enjoy the least
- **3 minutes**: Assign roles based on this conversation and record them in the group contract

In this ten-minute protocol, your learners can practice listening and speaking in a fairly low-risk environment. You will likely have a couple of groups that will need some help making a final decision on roles, but 80 percent of your groups will have no problem with this protocol, and roles will be decided.

Listing contact information might seem like a small thing, but it can do wonders for problem-solving when groups must work through absences and sharing data. Most learners do not have a problem sharing contact information, and I have many examples of win stories from this simple addition to the group contract. This also teaches learners how to be proactive. When teaching the group contract, you can give examples of when contact information may be helpful. See Win Story #2 at the end of this chapter as one of those examples.

The next part of the group contract, a firing clause, is not the immediate out that most learners want it to be. In the business world, it is challenging to fire someone for not doing their job well, and the same should be true in your groups. If a learner is brought to the teacher's attention for firing, there should be a teacher-led mediation, a redefining of roles, and action items with due dates to ensure that the individual in question has every opportunity to redeem themselves. The firing process can be a learning experience for everyone, but very few learners should get the ax! Logistically, you also need to think through what a learner would do after they are fired. How would you give them an opportunity to learn the standards outside of a group? It's a long, deep rabbit hole when firing someone. I recommend you keep it in a group contract but use it very sparingly.

Finally, every contract should have a place for learners to apply their signature. Ample emphasis should be used when teaching this part of the contract to explain how signing a contract is a promise. When we sign a contract, our character is on the line, and it means we agree to the terms listed. You may need to do a quick workshop on how to write your signature, which has real-world value for the rest of their lives. The signature lines provide a good vehicle to talk about living up to a standard of high character. You will be surprised how many of your learners appreciate and live up to that standard.

"When you need to innovate, you need collaboration."
~ Marissa Mayer

Group Meetings

Beginning and ending meetings can be another excellent accountability tool for group work. Effective group meetings are organized, short, and specific. The goal of a group meeting at the beginning of a work time is to establish what each member of the group will be working on. The expectations should be very clear about everything from what will be produced to the time it will take to create the work.

The goal of a group meeting at the end of a work time is to summarize completed work and establish next steps. End-of-class group meetings will let everyone see how they are contributing, discover where they need to focus their energy next, and provide you a view of where each group is. One of the roles you outline for each group will likely be a Recorder, and the Recorder can fill out a daily group sheet with updates from each group member in the last five minutes of class and report any issues to you that may require follow-up.

The group roles defined in the contract can be crucial for making sure everyone has work to do. Possible roles include: Leader, Technology Guru, Organizer, Researcher, Recorder, Teacher Liaison, Rubric Guru, etc. You can come up with an endless list of roles, but the real key is in how you define each role.

Another successful meeting tactic is to hold workshops specifically for each group role and then have them report back to their respective groups. For instance, have all the Technology Gurus report to a fifteen-minute workshop in which you teach them how to operate a specific function on Google Drive. At the conclusion of the workshop, have the concrete next steps for the Technology Gurus to report back to their group. Assigning specific workshops for each role allows you to more evenly distribute the workload amongst the learners in each group.

Decision Matrix

To equip learners with the skills to pick the best solution to the problem they are addressing, you will need to scaffold the process. A Decision Matrix is a great way to help the problem-solving process become less emotional and more logical. The purpose of a Decision Matrix is to ensure every learner's voice is valued and have each learner's idea evaluated on the criteria most important to the project goal. Your learners can get too attached to their ideas and might have a hard time letting them go. On the flip side, your learners also may not want to hurt anyone's feelings, so they might include everybody's idea even if it doesn't actually help solve the real-world problem. The Decision Matrix will give the group quantifiable numbers through a more logical process to help them choose a single solution to move forward with.

Admittedly, the numbers do have a personal connection to the learner to some degree since they are being assigned by learners with different viewpoints, but each learner must commit to a number and then be able to explain why they selected that number. The result is often the most organized and logical conversation the learners have ever had. Just like the structure of a group contract, learners will appreciate having a means to help with the decision of which solution to move forward with in Step 5.

To create a Decision Matrix, you need to determine the most important aspects of the PBL Unit from your rubric. In the blank Decision Matrix below, there are spaces for four solution criteria. Using your rubric in Step 2, each learners' possible solution will be given a score based on how well it meets your solution criteria. After each group member's solution is given a score for each of the solution criteria, the group can total up the scores to see which idea best addresses the rubric. The wording and process are important here.

The group is looking for *the idea* that best helps solve the problem. The group is not judging *the person*. With the Decision Matrix, we help learners collaborate to find the best solution regardless of who came up with the idea. The numbering system in conjunction with the rubric lets the learners decide in a logical and less emotional way which ideas to move forward with. And as the teacher, you are glad to see your groups making decisions based on your guidance through the rubric, which ensures your groups are headed in the right direction. The blank Decision Matrix below is a template you can customize for your own PBL Unit.

Decision Matrix					
	Solution Criteria 1	Solution Criteria 2	Solution Criteria 3	Solution Criteria 4	Total Score
Option 1					
Option 2					
Option 3					
Option 4					
Group Choice 1: _____					
Group Choice 2: _____					
Group Choice 3: _____					
Group Choice 4: _____					

Completing the Decision Matrix

Let's look at a completed Decision Matrix to see how the process plays out in real life. You have the structure to help groups make a logical decision, but how do you get them to share their ideas and fill out the Decision Matrix? My answer is typically a structured protocol, but then again, I use structured protocols to have my kids share about their day at the dinner table.

Below is an example of a protocol you can run with groups to help them fill out their Decision Matrix. As with any protocol, feel free to modify it as you see ways to improve the process for your learners.

- **Partner 1** (2 min): Shares their solution, addressing the four main solution criteria listed on the Decision Matrix, while other group members listen and assign scores for each solution criteria.
- **Partners 2, 3, 4** (1 min): Ask clarifying questions about the solution to clear up any unclear details.
- **Partners 2, 3, 4** (2 min): "I likes"—Group members talk about what they like about the presented idea.
- Rotate through this five-minute protocol with each group member until everyone has shared.

At the conclusion of the twenty-minute protocol, give your groups another five minutes to discuss what they heard and agree on the final numbers for their Decision Matrix. You may need to give yourself and learners a bit more time the first time you use a Decision Matrix, but once your learners are accustomed to the process, the Decision Matrix can save you a lot of time and build a positive, collaborative culture. Using a Decision Matrix helps your learners learn how to communicate professionally, think critically, problem-solve, and work in a team. These are the skills employers want our learners to have as they head into the workforce. In your classroom, you want your learners to have these skills because it empowers them to solve their own problems and those of others. You are creating a culture in which you no longer have to solve every problem.

Decision Matrix					
	Solution Criteria 1 Community Partner Interaction	**Solution Criteria 2** Explanation of Social Construction Experiment	**Solution Criteria 3** Use of Technology	**Solution Criteria 4** End Product Creativity	**Total Score**
Sara's Solution	5	3	2	4	14
Ryan's Solution	1	2	5	2	10
Lakshmi's Solution	5	5	1	5	16
Tate's Solution	4	4	2	3	13

Group Choice 1: Lakshmi's Solution with Ryan's Technology Idea

Group Choice 2: Sara's Solution with Ryan's Technology Idea

Group Choice 3: Tate's Solution with Ryan's Technology Idea and Lakshmi's End Product Idea

Group Choice 4: Ryan's Solution with Sara's Community Partner Idea and Lakshmi's Social Construction Experiment Idea

From the completed Decision Matrix above, a group can make a data-based decision about which solution to move forward with for Step 5. This group may decide to move forward with Lakshmi's overall solution since her solution has the highest total score. They may also decide that even though Ryan's solution scored the lowest overall, he does seem to have a uniquely positive idea when it comes to the technology portion of this PBL Unit.

In the end, we hope to at least create a structured environment to help learners have a positive, collaborative conversation. In the resources section, I list a blog post that explains more about a Decision Matrix if you would like more information.

Fishbowl

Of all the steps in the PBL process, Step 4: Pick a Solution is the most foreign to learners, so every portion of Step 4 should be modeled for learners the first time. When we model a protocol or new idea for learners, we call it a fishbowl protocol. In a fishbowl protocol, you and a small group of prepped learners are the fish while the rest of the class is on the outside of the fishbowl observing.

A fishbowl protocol is a great way to introduce new concepts such as a group meeting. To run a fishbowl protocol for a group meeting, you and three learners model for the class the appropriate way to run a group meeting. The teacher and the group are "in the fishbowl," and the rest of the class is watching specific members of the group. The group acts as if they are the only ones in the room and work through their meetings while the rest of the class watches. In the end, the whole class can debrief the strengths and weaknesses of the group meeting shown in the fishbowl. This fishbowl protocol allows learners to see what successful implementation looks like and gives you a means to bring learners back to a shared experience. For example, "Remember in the fishbowl when we established laptops should be closed in a group meeting? Please close your laptops for your group meetings."

Grouping Conclusion

Groups may seem like a lot of work at this point, but they have a lot of upsides for our learners. The ability to work in a group is listed as a key component of success by workforce leaders.[3] Whether our learners are headed straight to the workforce or into a post-second-ary opportunity, working in a group is going to be a skill they need in their toolbox. To provide opportunities for our learners, we must help them understand how to work in a group. Adding structure and process to groups will help turn the past mess of groups into a future of collaborative success.

Win Story #1

Dante: "Our contract says we can fire people, so we want to fire Jason."

Me: "Your contract does say you can fire people. Your contract also states you must have evidence for firing, and your group has to go through a mediation process with me."

Dante: "He doesn't do anything, so we want to fire him. Will you go tell him he is fired?"

Me: "Probably not, but why don't you tell your group to come over here so we can talk about some of the issues you all are having?"

The above dialogue doesn't sound like much of a win, but having been through many group mediations and only firing one learner, I can tell you these mediations are where most of the productive learning around how to act in a group comes from. Let me give you some dialogue from a group mediation session:

(All three learners look upset, so I am overly cheery.)

Me: "Thanks for coming over. I hear you may be having a bit of a misunderstanding within your group."

All three learners: "Well, he . . . " and "She said . . . " and "We want to fire . . . "

Me: "Let's do this a bit differently. I'd like to run a quick protocol. Let's give everyone some uninterrupted time to tell us about what they see and feel as well as some possible solutions. Dante, you brought this to my attention, so why don't you and Alise start. You have one minute. The rest of us are just going to listen."

Dante: "Well, like I said before, Jason isn't doing any work, so we want to fire him."

Me: "Is there anything else you want to say? You still have forty-five seconds. Alise, do you want to add anything?"

Dante/Alise: "Nope."

Me: "Jason, how about you?"

Jason: "I don't know what I am supposed to do. They just did a bunch of work without talking to me and then told me to 'start doing some work.' I would do some work, but they just keep getting an attitude, so then I didn't want to do anything."

Me: "Thanks, Jason. Do you have any ideas for a solution?"

Jason: "Nope."

Me: "Well, I see a couple of possible solutions. Dante and Alise, do you have some specific tasks you would like Jason to help with?"

Alise: "Yeah, I guess he could research the effects of hemophilia on younger kids so that we could put it in our Public Service Announcement."

Me: "Jason, do you think you could do that? If yes, when do you think you could have that done by?"

Jason: "I could probably get that done by the end of the period, or I can have it ready by tomorrow morning."

Me: "Dante and Alise, does that work on your end?"

Dante/Alise: "Sure."

Me: "Alright! Let's all check in quickly at the beginning of the period tomorrow to make sure everything is copacetic."

(Sometimes using big words at the end of mediation confuses teenagers and lightens the mood.)

Critical Components of a Group

Mediation:

- Use a protocol that involves several rounds of individuals talking or responding without interruption, which lets everyone's voice be heard.
- Make the next steps clear with a due date.
- Check in to make sure the next steps are completed.
- Have a separate one-on-one check-in if necessary to make sure everyone is alright.
- Trust me, spending the five to seven minutes in group mediation is well worth it.

Win Story #2

Samuel was unexpectedly sick just days before a big group presentation. As the Organizer in the group, he had access to all the group's work. Unfortunately, the group had not thought through the idea of accessing their work in Samuel's absence. In past years, I likely would have had three people sitting around for forty-eight minutes whining about not having any work to do every time I pushed them. Since they had a group contract with contact information, the group had already contacted Samuel in an earlier class period to get access to their work, and Samuel did a video call during their class period to help with some direction.

Fail Story #1

Fail stories in groups are not hard to find, and you likely have your own. Here are a few common group work failures you may be trying to avoid:

- Strong academic learner does all the work
- Group members do the jobs individually and then just mash everything together without any real collaboration
- Group members just talk
- Introverted members do not interact
- Accountability for grades gets tricky

Fail Story #2

During a school visit, I saw Mr. Stevens helping his class define their roles. The most popular role was Group Leader, which I thought was interesting because this is often a role with a lot of responsibility and a heavier workload. The groups fought over and heatedly debated why they wanted to be the group leader. After some discussion, all was decided, and the groups started their work. As the groups started working, one young Group Leader brazenly put his feet up on the desk with his hands behind his head. As an active observer, I went over and asked him if he was done with his work already. I was surprised to hear him explain with all honesty that he was doing it, "I'm the boss. I get to sit around and tell people what to do."

Now I knew why so many learners wanted to be the Group Leader. The perception was that the Group Leader was the boss who sat around bossing people around and not doing any work. Mr. Stevens brought everyone together and had a very helpful discussion about servant leadership. Some groups reworked their roles and started their PBL Unit again.

Bottom Line #1: Step 4 should establish groups and a single solution for the group to work toward in Step 5.

Bottom Line #2: Groups are hard even for adults, so it will take intentional work to make sure groups are thriving. It is worth it!

Where to Start

Group contracts and a decision matrix will give groups structure. Structure is key to group success. Lunchrooms often lack structure or purpose; thus, while the learners are technically in groups, very little good comes from the interactions. Start with a group contract template and then customize it to meet your specific needs. Look for a group contract that gives everyone in the group a role. A role ensures everyone has a job to do and makes the accountability for that role much more concrete.

Resources

All resources listed can be found at:
www.magnifylearningin.org/pbl-simplified-book-resources.

- Group Contracts and Groups
- *PBL Simplified* Video Series—Group Contracts
- Decision Matrix

Questions

- What types of groupings have worked for you in the past? Random? Groups of two, three, or four?
- What is your favorite group project? Why do you appreciate it so much?
- Ask your learners what they like and dislike about group work.

CHAPTER 6

Step 5: Create, Run, and Inspect Solution

"Dream, struggle, create, prevail. Be daring.
Be brave. Be loving. Be compassionate.
Be strong. Be brilliant. Be beautiful."
~ Caterina Fake

Step 5 is a weighty step. You have worked through establishing and teaching useful group work. Groups will still need to be mediated throughout Step 5, but you have already modeled successful groups and set up contracts for each group. Success is imminent! It is time to put those groups to work.

In Step 5, learners will test their solution to the problem from the Entry Event. Hopefully, and most likely, the solution will fail! TED Talks and blogs tell us that failing is a great tool, but what does that mean exactly? As seen in the Decision Matrix, the answer from any one learner is likely not going to completely solve the real-world problem, so learners may end up using different parts of each group member's ideas. Essentially, everyone's idea failed in some form right off the bat based on their Decision Matrix scores, and that is good! It is a great time to teach your learners about perseverance and revising work to make a better product.

Once groups have a reasonable solution to the real-world problem, it is time to test it. An idea should be tested several times before the final presentation. A Tuning Protocol is a great way to test an idea in a very low-risk environment focused on feedback rather than evaluation.

Tuning Protocol Example

- **Partner A (2 min):** Present idea to share
- **Partners B, C (1 min):** Clarifying questions
- **Partners B, C (2 min):** "I like"
- **Partners B, C (2 min):** "I wonder"
- **Partners A (1 min):** Reflection on the feedback

The above Tuning Protocol is meant to be modified to fit different contexts, but it proves to be very effective for both adults and learners. Similar to the Decision Matrix process in Chapter 5, you are helping learners tune the *idea*, not judge the person, which is the secret sauce of protocols. The above format gives a lot of feedback to the presenting partners, and the other partners get to hear quality ideas as they give feedback. Here are a few key points to remember as you try out a Tuning Protocol:

- Time constraints are helpful for creativity
- Times can be adjusted depending on the purpose and available times

- Shorter time frames might be helpful for those new to Tuning Protocols
- Clarifying questions are typically short answers or yes/no
- While learners will eventually be able to run Tuning Protocols by themselves, you should be the timekeeper to start out
- As the facilitator of the Tuning Protocol, I have run this with very large groups
- The wording of "I like" and "I wonder" is important
  - "I like how you differentiated the end product for learners."
  - "I like how your Entry Event is tied to your community partner."
  - "I wonder if your community partner could be someone from the local history museum."
  - "I wonder if you have thought about partnering with third grade since they also touch on those standards."

Feedback—You Can't Do It Alone!

An important note should be made about feedback here as Tuning Protocols are introduced. Ron Berger from Expeditionary Learning has a great video about feedback. You can find it by googling "Austin's Butterfly," and it shows learners the power of peer feedback that is "kind, helpful, and specific." Timely would be another excellent adjective to add to that list. The power of feedback, and the necessity of empowering your learners to give good feedback, cannot be overstated.

Feedback teaches our learners to be reflective and multiplies your impact. One of the most powerful gifts we can give any learner is the ability to reflect and make changes. For the immediate future, giving and receiving feedback in a school setting is helpful for creating an end product and solution for the immediate problem in our

PBL Unit, but feedback and reflection are also skills our learners will use after they have left our classrooms. We want our learners to be able to evaluate their relationships, jobs, and life situations in a way that shows them new opportunities and provides the best possible future for them. See Win Story #2 of this chapter as an example of how these PBL skills help learners build skills for future success.

Most likely, your "why" for teaching is more connected to your learners' overall life success than mastery of your content standards. We use our content standards and Project Based Learning as vehicles to help our learners see opportunities they may not have seen otherwise, and feedback is a great example of a lifelong skill that can be developed to create success well beyond school.

Feedback through a Tuning Protocol will multiply your impact in the classroom. If you have a class with thirty learners and you give them all two minutes of feedback, it will take you a full hour, and that's only if you don't have any interruptions or time in transition. With interruptions and transitions, it likely would take you three class periods! If your learners are taught how to give kind, specific, and helpful feedback, they can receive feedback simultaneously instead of chronologically from you. With the same class of thirty learners, you could run a Tuning Protocol in which every learner receives eight minutes of feedback, and you still finish in less than one class period. The power of collaborative feedback through a structured Tuning Protocol multiplies your classroom time, which is easily your most precious commodity in a classroom. With the extra time, you can give more direct attention to the learners who most need your help or develop deeper relationships with your learners. The Tuning Protocol gives learners the vocabulary they need to provide constructive feedback politely. By investing the time to teach the powerful skill of providing meaningful feedback early, a teacher can reap the benefits throughout the year.

"The goal of education is not to increase the amount of knowledge but to create the possibilities for a child to invent and discover, to create adults who are capable of doing new things."
~ Jean Piaget

Rubric Check & Practice Presentation

In Step 5, the group should do another ongoing reflective assessment against the rubric they received in Step 2. A possible group role (or even a rotating role) can be the Rubric Guru. The Rubric Guru goes through the rubric to make sure the group is on the right track. Rubric updates should be addressed at the beginning of group meetings to make sure the tasks the group is working on are relevant to the work they need to complete.

You may have a formal benchmark in Step 5 when groups turn in a highlighted rubric, so you can quickly get a visual of where the groups are in the process of solving their problem and preparing for their final presentation. As the final presentation approaches, you want to make sure you don't have any groups heading off track. A practice presentation can be another formal check for progress as the last benchmark before a final presentation. Practice presentations serve a variety of critical purposes:

- Show learners where they are missing key components
- Give everyone a practice stress event
- Allow the teacher to hear and see what learners will be presenting
- Add another benchmark besides the final presentation

The critical logistical consideration for practice presentations is to provide enough revision days between a practice presentation and the final presentation. With at least one revision day between the practice presentation and the final presentation, your learners can fix any last-minute issues. To find out presentations have deficiencies during a practice round without allowing time for learners to fix them is a futile practice.

Practice presentations show learners what they need to work on—a hook that involves a play that the group planned on winging doesn't look so great when performed, a budget that has to go on a projection screen needs another revision to make sure the numbers match up, etc. A friendly practice presentation is a great time to fail because there is still time to revise and prepare for success before the final presentation in front of community partners. Learners can have a great plan in their head as they think about what they will say to the crowd, but these plans are often harder to pull off when they have to actually present it. A practice presentation with the audience looking at different portions of the rubric helps draw out the key components that are either shining or missing.

Plus, stress can be a good thing! When a class seems to be downplaying or missing the immediacy of a project, you may want to bump up practice presentations even earlier. Practice presentations can be a great way to show groups that they have a lot of work to do. Again, even without being apathetic, learners can feel that they are prepared when they have an enormous amount of work to do. Practice presentations can serve as an excellent temperature check for groups.

One of my favorite parts of PBL is having learners present their final presentations to authentic audiences of community partners.

It raises the bar for learners and gives them a chance to shine in front of professionals who don't know the great things that are happening in your classroom; however, it is imperative that you know what your learners are going to say beforehand. Are they prepared? Are their facts way off? Does everyone get to talk? Do they go off on a tangent and present something weird? Having the practice presentation several days before the final presentation polishes the presentations and gives you peace of mind knowing exactly what the community partners will see and hear.

Presentation Day

Presentation day is an exciting day, and it should be marketed as such. Yes, marketed! You need to sell the awesomeness of presentations to your learners. For example, you can say things like:

- "Isn't it awesome that a real bank CEO is going to hear your idea?"
- "Can you believe you get to present your architecture plan to a real architect?"
- "I can't wait for you all to share your hard work with our panel of community partners!"

Now you have excited learners! So, what happens next?

Let's talk about the learner side first. The mini bottom line here is to make sure your learners are prepared, which admittedly is a massive task. Learners need to be ready with sufficient content mastery and presentation skills. Step 3 should have shown you where your learners are regarding content mastery, so in this chapter, I focus on presentation skills.

"Repetition doesn't create memories. New experiences do."
~ Brian Chesky

Your learners will not intrinsically know what an excellent presentation looks like or how they should act during one, so you need to set up some scaffolding opportunities for them to learn the process we likely take for granted. For example, one of my favorite workshops of all time is the handshake workshop. We take for granted that learners know how to give a good firm handshake when meeting a community partner. A quick fifteen-minute workshop can outline the difference between the long, creepy handshake, dead fish, and a firm, professional handshake. It makes a huge, long-lasting difference as our learners look to move toward opportunities in the professional world. One study showed that employers make a decision about an interview candidate within the first five minutes of an interview.[4] Someone's handshake, eye contact, and body language often make a bigger impression than their responses to interview questions.

A professional dress workshop can be a game changer for learners as well. What does it look like for learners to dress up for a presentation? It makes a big difference in how learners see themselves, and community partners will always notice. While many learners do not think it should matter what you wear to an interview or to the bank, how we present ourselves does matter. We want to equip our learners with tips that apply to the professional world to best prepare them to be successful there. For some learners, dressing up means wearing a dress suit or tie while for others it means wearing a polo shirt. The important concept that you want learners to take from this workshop is that there is a difference when you dress up in how you hold yourself and the impression you make. I've even seen schools that create a professional dress closet for learners in case they do not yet have professional clothes. There are many creative ways to help our learners confidently present and see themselves in professional work in the future.

Having a presentation rubric is also a great way to communicate your expectations to your learners. There are resources listed at the end of this chapter that provide some examples of presentation rubrics, but two important notes on rubrics in general are to: 1) make sure learners receive the rubric at the beginning of the project so they can ask Need to Knows and 2) make sure you don't grade anything you haven't taught. By having a presentation rubric, your learners can ask for presentation workshops at the very beginning of the PBL Unit if they feel that is a Need to Know. Having a presentation rubric early also allows learners to get an idea of what their final presentation will look like and helps them ask questions about presenting they would not have thought to ask otherwise. For example, including a line that requires 85 percent eye contact with the audience lets your learners know they will not just be reading off slides during the presentation. The consistent communication of presentation expectations begins to build your culture of excellence in this area.

Another way to help our learners understand what a powerful presentation looks and sounds like is to watch excellent presentations and have learners identify key attributes for effective presentations from them. Select powerful TED Talks on important subjects you want to expose your learners to and have them identify what makes each of these talks so powerful.

Chapter 11 is on grading, but it is important to note here that we cannot grade our learners on excellent presentation skills if we have not taught them excellent presentation skills. When we expect learners to give 85 percent eye contact to the audience, but they have never had a workshop for this skill, we create an unrealistic expectation. A short workshop on giving eye contact allows us to show examples, present skills, and give learners time to practice this skill. After the workshop, you can grade this skill and give feedback individually to help each learner grow.

There are also a few logistical scaffolding pieces for final presentations you may want to consider:

- Presentation schedule
- Sample questions community partners might ask
- Feedback sheet for community partners

A key to freeing your learners from the fear associated with presenting is to shed as much light on the process as you can. You should post a presentation schedule as soon as you can or at least a few days before presentation day so learners can see when they are presenting. When learners know when they will be presenting, they can start to prepare themselves mentally and emotionally for their presentations. They know how much extra time they have or do not have, whether they have to be first, etc.

Community partners are going to be an asset in ramping up the authenticity and importance of your presentations. At the same time, we do not want our learners freaking out because they have a stranger in the classroom for their presentation. Providing learners with some sample questions community partners might ask is a helpful scaffolding piece and can be as simple as an Exit Ticket leading up to presentation day. Have learners answer some of the sample questions below:

- "Why did you pick this project idea?"
- "What was the most challenging part of the project?"
- "What is your favorite part of the project?"
- "If I am going to remember one thing from your presentation, what should it be?"
- "Who else should hear the information in this presentation?"
- "If you could redo one portion of your solution, what would you revise?"

You might take this same list of sample questions and include them on your community partner feedback sheet. When a community partner asks a question your learners are prepared for, it will be a big confidence booster for them. A community partner feedback sheet is important for making your community partner feel at ease as well. For some of your community partners, it's been a long time since they have been in a classroom, and even though they might run board meetings, they can be uncomfortable giving feedback to your learners. Community partners want to help by asking questions, but they don't want to make anyone cry. The feedback sheet makes the community partners feel like they are helping, and your learners will take their feedback very seriously. A simple feedback form of "I like" and "I wonder" is a useful tool to provide community partners along with your sample questions. It is open-ended enough for any community partner to give feedback no matter their background, and it is simple enough that your community partner will not feel overwhelmed. One fear a community partner might have is that they might not be helpful. Handing a community partner a full content-specific rubric can backfire because your community partner will be overwhelmed and won't get to enjoy the presentations. Let them enjoy their time with your learners, and let your learners enjoy sharing their work. Make presentation day a celebration of their work, not a speech they dread.

Win Story #1

This win story is really a turnaround story that shows the power of the process of empowering learners. During a presentation with a community partner from the largest children's museum in the world in the audience, a learner named Sam used a racial slur. Yep. Remember, you can't really teach them when they are presenting. All you can do is listen . . . and sometimes try to hide.

To make this a win story, I must share the full growth mindset side of the story. The next year, Sam looked at his presentations differently. Sam was engaged in the PBL process and appreciated the culture. His presentation win came during a presentation involving the Civil War. In full costume, Sam presented well-thought-out ideas to a professional audience. Sam shook people's hands before and after the presentation with a newfound confidence. Sam had the opportunity to define a new life for himself that is much different than the one he had experienced thus far.

Win Story #2

The skill of giving and receiving feedback builds our learners' ability to look at their current situation and make adjustments instead of just accepting what is given to them. Simon, who is featured in a win story in Chapter 3, was the learner with the lowest score in the school. After being in a Project Based Learning classroom, he learned more than content standards. Simon took a job as a package handler—a good move since it comes with benefits and a decent starting wage. Simon has learned to reflect and not be content with his first iteration of life though. He noticed that if you get a forklift certification, you get more pay, have more job security, and have a more diverse work shift. Simon realized there was more opportunity in his current situation with additional learning, so he went for it. College wasn't his area of interest, but he didn't see that as a failure. He saw his situation as a place that could always be improved through continuous learning and refinement. He now has added a hazmat certification for more pay and job security, which his wife appreciates. Project Based Learning and its benefits matter to all of our learners!

Fail Story

Before I was doing practice presentations, I had a learner we'll call Rudy. Rudy was from a pretty rough family situation and was behind academically, but he did work for me and tried most of the time. For one workshop, we were sharing poetry in the old-fashioned presentation format to our peers. It was primarily original poetry, so I had given many talks about being kind to others and being great listeners. Rudy was up, and I gave him an affirming look and asked him to come forward. Rudy stepped up to the podium with notes in hand, and we put on our best listening ears. The problem was that Rudy opened his mouth, and no sound came out. I calmly affirmed him and told him to take a step back and then start as soon as he was ready. Two attempts, and still no words. Not even a stutter! Unfortunately, a young lady in the front squeezed out the smallest giggle—not a mean cackle, but an unintentional giggle. Rudy responded by flipping the entire class the bird with both hands and then walked out. We all sat stunned. As I reflect and write, I am slammed in the face by the awful situation I put Rudy in. I put him in a fight-or-flight situation. Would a practice presentation have helped? I think so. Rudy could have practiced the stressful situation, and I would have known what he was planning.

Bottom Line: Make the work public. Make the work exciting!

Where to Start

Instead of having your learners present to only you and their peers, invite a community partner. If the community partner is relevant to the topic you are studying, it is a bonus, but if you can't find the exact professional you are looking for, find any professional who can give feedback on the presentations of your learners. Bringing in someone from outside of school ramps up the intensity of your presentations. It is often acceptable and sometimes even "cool" to give an awful presentation to your peers and teacher. Apathetic presentations are much harder to pull off when the audience includes a banker, an architect, and a small business owner.

Resources

All resources listed can be found at:
www.magnifylearningin.org/pbl-simplified-book-resources.

- Feedback and Revision
  - Ideas for feedback
- Austin's Butterfly YouTube Video
- Presentation Rubric

Questions

- Are you worried about your learners failing? Why or why not?
- When is it okay for learners to fail?

- What community partners can you invite to a presentation day?
- When can you insert a Tuning Protocol?

CHAPTER 7

Step 6: Reflect on Solution

"Experience is not the best teacher; evaluated experience is the best teacher. Reflective thinking is needed to turn experience into insight."
~ John Maxwell

Reflection on learning should be happening throughout the project by asking learners for feedback about the effectiveness of workshops, processes, groups, and community partners. By asking learners to reflect and provide feedback, we show respect for their voice, improve your work as an educator, and differentiate the classroom. Reflection on and celebration of the whole PBL Unit are also good ways to bring closure to the current PBL Unit before beginning another.

As you help your learners move from a passive role to an empowered role through Project Based Learning, continuous reflection is a major contributor to that transformation. By asking your learners to reflect and provide feedback on *your* work, you are giving them a voice they do not typically get. In a typical classroom, a learner is rarely asked if they have ideas for how to improve their classroom. When you are vulnerable and confident enough to ask, "What did you like about this unit?" and "What do you think we can improve on?", these two questions can invite your learners to be active participants in building your culture and guiding their own learning.

As you read this book, listen to the *PBL Simplified* Podcast, and watch the *PBL Simplified* Video Series if you are looking to improve your skillset as an educator. Thank you for your dedication to the craft of teaching. Teaching is a calling, and you want to be at your best. Asking your learners to reflect and give you feedback is just another way to level up your teaching. You are serving your learners, so who better to receive feedback from to help you improve? For example, you might ask, "I think this protocol really helped you all have a professional conversation. How do you think we can improve it for next time?"

Reflection can also be a way to help differentiate the learning. Have your learners reflect on *how* they learn as well as what they learned. You may find you have a subset of learners who appreciate learning visually, so you might add Khan Academy videos as additional scaffolding for them. As you empower your learners to be reflective, you may be surprised by the insights they have into their learning styles.

"By three methods we may learn wisdom: First, by reflection, which is noblest; Second, by imitation, which is easiest; and third, by experience, which is the bitterest."

~ Confucius

How to Reflect

Now that I've talked about the "why" for reflection and its many benefits, let's walk through a few reflection methods that work well in Project Based Learning.

The first is an Exit Ticket. Exit Tickets asking learners for an "I like" and an "I wonder" can reveal a lot about how the overall project is going and can take as little as three minutes at the end of a class period or workshop. Your Exit Ticket can be as simple as a post-it note they leave on the wall as they exit the classroom or a quick Google Form before they log off. You are left with a list of "I likes" telling you what you should continue and a list of "I wonders" giving you suggestions for improvement.

A Chalk Talk protocol from the School Reform Initiative can be an efficient way to get quick, meaningful feedback. During a Chalk Talk, learners look at and comment on a specific phrase or question posed by the facilitator either on a chalkboard, dry erase board, or piece of chart paper. Then the learners silently write down their thoughts. Learners can comment on the thoughts of other learners to create a type of classroom mind map. It's a conversation that takes place on paper instead of with words. Can you think of some potential wins in this process for some of your learners? Do you have any introverted learners? Any learners who may need to practice thinking before they answer? With a little practice, learners come to love the protocol as a way to see what others are thinking and have their ideas publicly displayed.

Golden Shining Moments is another protocol that shares successes and builds momentum. Golden Shining Moments asks learners to focus on the great things they experienced during a PBL Unit—everything from a community partner interaction to rocking their presentation. Give learners dry erase markers and let them reflect on the best portions of the project by writing thoughts on the board (not by talking). Allow them to "+1" someone else's idea if they agree, and watch the different positives start to multiply.

In a different vein, Roses, Thorns, and Buds will give you a more balanced view of how things are going. Learners share on a post-it note or Chalk Talk the warm feedback (roses), the cool feedback (thorns), and a good idea for next time (buds). If you use post-it notes, have learners begin to group their ideas and see where patterns emerge.

These are just a few ways to include learners in the reflection process. The methods abound, and a quick internet search will load you up with a plethora of ideas for reflection, so begin collecting—and implementing—your favorites.

While reflection happens throughout the project, there is value in devoting a day to reflect and celebrate. Presentation day is a celebration while sharing the deliverable with a community partner, but reflection day can be a time to reflect and celebrate the class. As you start out, know that many learners have never been part of such an authentic and meaningful project, so it is important to commend learners on the challenging work they have undertaken.

Invite community partners into the reflection by asking them for feedback and testimonials of their experience. Sharing outside reflection on the learners' good work can carry a lot of weight as you build your positive, collaborative culture. A community partner may have mentioned how they were impressed with learners' deep knowledge of the subject or how professionally a group presented. Public praise is always a big self-esteem booster, so this may be a good time to highlight a few learners who may not always shine in an academic setting. Recognition from a community partner goes a long way, so it is essential to give the community partner an opportunity to provide that praise.

While the praise for and acknowledgment of the learners' hard work are essential, we also want to use this time to improve and demonstrate our growth mindset. Groups may need this opportunity to enhance their project if they still need to implement it in the community. Ask learners what workshops they may still need based on feedback from the community partners or to help them prepare for the next presentation. As you are looking for improvements, it is vital for you to put yourself out there as well and ask learners what you can do to improve for the next project (and what you did well). There is a risk as we put our PBL Unit out there for feedback, but this is the perfect time to show that we are also working with a growth mindset. A protocol and careful planning are helpful here to make sure that the session is productive and goes well. Asking the class of thirty teenagers how the project went with no structure is not going to get you the feedback you desire. Here are some questions to consider as you create a time of reflection:

- How can you make sure everyone's voice is heard?
- How do you make sure overly negative or positive voices don't take over the time?
- How will you respond to the feedback? (Hint: You don't have to respond immediately.)
- How can you help scaffold the process for learners who have never given feedback to a facilitator?

The last thing you want is a negative free-for-all led by a few strong voices. The second-to-last thing you want is to be defensive as the feedback comes out. It is appropriate to ask clarifying questions about the learner feedback, and you may have some factors that are forcing your hand such as a district timeline or mandate. You still want to be professional, calm, and open to the learners' feedback. However the feedback comes from learners, you will want to thank them for offering their suggestions and note that you will take them into consideration.

Once you have received feedback from your learners, you want to act on some portion of the feedback as soon as you can. Even if it is a relatively small aspect, when you act on the feedback learners have given, you are building trust and respect because they see through your actions that you have heard their voice. Learners are not accustomed to adults listening to their voice. Valuing learners' voices begins to build their confidence and is a major tool in moving learners out of the spoon-fed zone and into a zone of empowerment, pride, and self-motivation.

 "The real man smiles in trouble, gathers strength from distress, and grows brave by reflection."
~ Thomas Paine

As you develop a toolbox for reflection—throughout each project and as a final step—you will be modeling a growth mindset for your learners. Be open with this process. Share any immediate changes you make along with changes throughout the years based on previous learner reflections. You might say, "Based on your reflections from the last project, we are going to take less time during Need to Knows in the next project." Connecting the dots for learners is an essential step in making sure they understand how much you value their voice.

Win Story

We often talk about how failure is a positive, so this story is about how I was able to turn the Fail Story below into a Win Story (feel free to read the Fail Story first!). The day after my class had some reflection time, based on a tip from a learner, I used a more differentiated and concrete process to determine individual understanding. I would ask the same question about a given Need to Know, but this time, I asked each learner to place a hand over their heart with a number from one to five. One meant that they needed another workshop and five said they had mastered the content. Holding a number in front of their chest gave them an anonymous way to ask for help. The second round did not move as many of the Need to Knows over as I was hoping, but it gave me a much better assessment of the needs of my learners. We ran additional workshops for those who needed them to save the day, but I almost missed a significant portion of learning because I chose a reflection activity that did not meet the needs of my situation. Did you notice the whole idea of using a finger reporting system came from a learner? Because I was transparent about not being confident I was getting true feedback, I had a learner help me out, and that learner helped me out because she cared about the success of *our* classroom.

Fail Story

While group shares are likely the easiest and most commonly used method of reflection, it can be difficult to make sure you are hearing everyone's voice. At the end of one class period, we were moving Need to Knows over to the Know side because we had performed a series of workshops. While I tried to use a "Thumbs up/Thumbs down" system to figure out whether we should move a topic over, I could tell I was not getting everyone to enthusiastically give me reflective feedback. I tried to ramp up my energy level and moved many of the topics over the Know side. I was too focused on being a facilitator rather than checking in with my learners and thought because I held a workshop on a topic that the learners had mastered the content. Workshops do not always equal mastery! We need to be data-driven to make sure we have mastery. If the data shows you need to hold another workshop, let's do that to serve our learners well.

> **Bottom Line: Reflection helps solidify the learning**
> **and prepare everyone for the next PBL Unit.**
> **Reflection should capture everyone's voice.**

Where to Start

Ask learners what they thought about your last PBL Unit. You need to help them a bit at first because they will not have language for this yet. Don't just ask the whole group either because you will likely only get crickets or hear a few strong voices, so find a protocol. A Chalk Talk about Golden Shining Moments and another for improvements would work well, or just ask learners to write down two things they liked about the last unit and two things they would change. The key to the whole process is to find one common thread to change and then change that right away. Then be public with your actions by saying something like, "Based on your feedback, you liked having a community partner in the presentation audience, so we are going to do that again. You also said you didn't like the way you were assigned a topic to research, so for this unit I am going to give you a list of topics to choose from."

Even if you get this wrong, learners will acknowledge that you are trying to listen to their voice. Attempting to listen to their voice gives them permission to provide you with more feedback on things they like or would like to see modified. It is empowering and part of the process of building a learner-centered classroom.

Resources

All resources listed can be found at:
www.magnifylearningin.org/pbl-simplified-book-resources.

- Reflection
    - Learner Reflection Resources
    - Teacher Reflection Example

Questions

- Reflect on your own teaching practice.
    - What do you like about your teaching?
    - What would you like to improve on?
- Be brave and ask learners what you do well as a teacher and what you could improve on.

CHAPTER 8

Community Partners

*"A good collaboration pushes
the boundaries of both partners."*
~ Neil Blumenthal

C ommunity partners are a vital piece of authentic Project Based Learning. If we want our learners to solve real-world problems, we need someone to introduce them to our learners. Who better to make the introduction than the community partners who are currently working to solve these real-world problems?

To find the right community partner for your PBL Unit, look at your standards and ask two questions:

1. Who cares about these standards and my learners?
2. Who is currently working with topics that apply this standard?

If you are looking at standards for investigating invasive species, these two questions will lead you to your local Department of Natural Resources and employees who are currently working to eradicate invasive species in your local state parks. The Department of Natural Resources in your area cares about eradicating invasive species and is currently involved in this work. If your standards are writing for a specific audience about voting rights, you might reach out to your local voting organizations. Voting organizations care about voting rights and are currently doing this work.

When you know you have a great PBL Unit idea, it can sometimes be a little abrupt to ask, "Who cares?", but it really is one of the best questions you can ask yourself to find a community partner. At Magnify Learning, we work with educators from across the country, and we find that everyone's standards have someone who cares about them out in the real world. You as the content expert are the perfect bridge between the classroom and the community partner who can package the real-world problem for your learners.

Community Partner Placement

Once you have identified a community partner to come in and bring authenticity to your PBL Unit, you must decide which part of your PBL Unit to invite them into. Community partners can be involved in any part of the PBL process, but some areas might require more from them than others. As you get started on your PBL journey, Entry Events and having community partners join presentation day to create authentic audiences are typically good starting points. Many organizations or industry partners have an outreach person on staff who is hired to talk to schools. Specifically, large museums and zoos have outreach departments designed to engage school-age learners, so when you call them, you are helping them fulfill their mission. Nonprofits are also designed in a way that gets their message out to the community, so they often have processes in place for employees to come out to schools and talk with learners. Most of the time, having a community partner come and launch your Entry Event is something that is already in their area of expertise and is a natural first step in their involvement.

As you incorporate more presentations into your classrooms with Project Based Learning, you will want to have an authentic audience for each one. I've used this term throughout the book, but the definition of an authentic audience is that it includes someone (or more than one someone) from outside of your classroom and school who will serve as your audience. Your learners are already accustomed to presenting to their peers and you for a grade. When you bring an outside community partner into the audience, you up the level of importance and authenticity for a presentation. You should let learners know from the very beginning of the Entry Event that community partners will attend the presentations. You can then carry the momentum of this authentic Entry Event throughout the PBL Unit by saying something like, "Remember, you want to add an extra layer of excellence and professionalism to your work because Mike from the Hemophilia Society will be coming back to hear your presentations." Not only can community partners in the audience help add a layer of authenticity to your presentations but it is also an easy beginning ask for a community partner.

Entry Events and presentation days are great times to bring in a new community partner because you are not asking too much of them. Community partners usually have no problem saying "yes" to an hour of their time, but you'll need a more established relationship when you start to ask for more time, preparation, and expertise. As you become more proficient in leveraging relationships with community partners, they can also become content experts. You can bring in an architect to teach AutoCAD or bring in a DNA specialist to talk about chromosomes when you are holding workshops in Step 3. While it's an advanced move that requires a good relationship with your community partner, having a community partner from a marketing agency come in and teach your learners about persuasion can be a very powerful addition to your workshops.

"Most of my best projects are the ones where the learning was profound, even if the community impact was less visible; I say less visible because that is the key descriptor, I believe. All of our projects have community impact."
~ Andrew Larson, veteran PBLer

A quick word of caution about community partners: they are not money! Sometimes we see an outside company, think about how we need things in our classrooms or schools, and think that surely they can help. While it may be true that they *could* help with the financial need you have, community partners are much more important than money. The presence of a community partner shows learners that the work they are creating is worth showing up for.

The key to all these community partner moves is relationship. Your relationship with community partners will determine how much you can ask of them and how much they are willing to do for your learners. Having relationships with community partners is the key to having them come back again and again. If you invite someone to your classroom and ask them for money, you're abusing the relationship. If you ask someone to come for eight hours on their first visit, you are probably harming that relationship. It is your job to bridge the gap and find a natural entry point for your community partner and not to wear out the same ones over and over. As I already mentioned, an easy entry point might be one hour of watching presentations or launching an Entry Event. The goal of this positive interaction is to create a relationship-building win.

You typically get a very positive reaction when you give community partners an easy entry point. Once they have interacted with your learners in a low-pressure situation, they see the great things that you are doing and know that you are going to value your relationship with them. After you've built up some relational equity, you can begin to ask them for more of the same or you can up the ask. If you asked a community partner to watch presentations the first time they visited, you might then ask them if you can take a field trip to their plant or their office. As you develop your relationship, you might then ask them to come and do some workshops. Everything depends on the link you and your classes build with community partners.

The real-life fail story below will display some common errors that can stop a relationship from forming or hinder forward progress, including thinking that anyone outside of the education world runs their lives by bells in four-minute increments.

Win Story

Susan is from a large school district that has a PBL track. As a facilitator who knows the advantages of community partners, she is always on the lookout for community partners. Susan has a wide web of community help to call upon when she is looking for authenticity to ramp up her classroom, and she was looking for first responders to help launch her next project. The standards and deliverables were all set up, but she still needed the perfect community partner to help launch it. While making a quick stop at McDonalds, she found herself waiting in line behind a police officer. Knowing the benefit a community partner gives to learners, Susan jumped into a two-minute conversation in a fast-food line and landed a community partner who was very willing to come to her classroom. As it turns out, the officer was already in an outreach position, so it was that officer's job to present in classrooms. What a win-win scenario!

Fail Story #1

I was working with Mrs. T, and she took the risk of inviting a community partner into her classroom. We made sure the plan was solid, and her learners prepared well. The community partner was going to come in for the first time to watch presentations and give professional feedback. When I went in to check on how things went, I was shocked to hear that Mrs. T was not happy at all with her experience. Here was our exchange:

> **Me:** "So, how did it go? Did it revolutionize your classroom?"

> **Mrs. T:** "No! It was awful! He didn't show!"

> **Me:** "He didn't show at all? Did he at least call?"

> **Mrs. T:** "Well, he did show up eventually. But he was late. I ended up with thirty seventh graders and no speaker."

> **Me:** "When did you ask him to come in?"

> **Mrs. T:** "Third period at 9:24. He didn't show up until 9:30!"

Did you see the translation issue? In Mrs. T's world, six minutes of unscheduled time with seventh graders means more gray hair. For her community partner, 9:24 means that she probably wants him there by 9:30. Outside of the education world, 9:24 and 9:30 mean the same thing.

The second most common error when inviting a community partner into a classroom is to assume they have been in a school environment since they graduated. You live in the world of school and have developed a different normal than most people. Community partners likely don't know your building layout and have never experienced a passing period as an adult. What do you think a community partner thinks when they see a middle-school passing period—chaos, fire, massive brawl, loose wild animals? Meanwhile, middle-school teachers think things are going smoothly. **Our community partners don't understand your normal.**

To make a community partner feel at ease as they enter the building, it is a professional touch to have a learner tour guide meet them. A learner tour guide can begin building the positive relationship with a community partner before they even get to your classroom. A firm handshake, smile, and background information on your class and the PBL Unit will begin to build relational equity. Your learners likely do not naturally know how to greet an outside guest, but a couple of quick training sessions during lunch will help them develop the skills they need to be a tour guide. Learner tour guides are building networking and presentation skills that will be necessary as they enter college and the workforce. A great way to test out your tour guide's skills is to have them practice with another teacher who is acting as if they are the guest. Literally start the practice session at the front office and have the learner(s) walk their practice guest all the way to your classroom. The practice will be worth it.

The third error we often make when we invite community partners into our classroom is the "no follow-up" mistake. After you and your learners have knocked it out of the park with a new community partner and are ready for your next partnership, don't forget to take time to thank your guest! A community partner is taking time out of their day to help invest in the future generation; they are making a philanthropic gesture. While they are not doing it for a thank you, it is nice to solidify their good citizen feeling with a thank-you letter. Not an email! When you visit the office of a community partner, you never see a thank you email printed and hanging on the wall, but you will often see a handwritten thank you. And following up with them doesn't always have to be a thank-you letter. You could also send an update on a project they were a part of or an especially exciting win you had with learners. Give the community partner as much of a win as you can.

Fail Story #2

We had a school ask us to come help them create engagement in their PBL Units. They had worked with another group to get started with PBL, and while this school had the structures and the vocabulary, they were not seeing the engagement from their learners they expected from Project Based Learning. The lack of engagement was a bit of a stumper at first because Project Based Learning is a great instructional model for moving learners from apathetic to engaged.

Before we flew out to their school, we asked them to send their project planning forms to us. It didn't take us long to see where the engagement issue was coming from. They had PBL Units centered around standards and interesting end products, but when we looked at their audiences, we saw the problem. Every one of their audiences was marked "Learners and Teacher." They did not have any outside community partners coming in for presentations. The lack of an authentic audience led to this fail.

You, as the educator, are very important to a learner. You take up about 184 days of their year and can build a relationship that helps learners thrive, but your learners also know that if they don't turn in their best work, you will still love them. This can lead to lackluster presentations. When I come in as a community partner with a shirt and tie, I am an unknown person who brings mystery and stress. Learners ask things like:

- "Why is he here?"
- "Is he going to be mean?"
- "Is he going to be nice?"
- "What will he say about my presentation?"

At the end of the presentations, you and your learners will appreciate this outside presence who can come in and give authentic feedback on learner work. It also tells learners that their work is so important that people will take time away from the rest of their job to come and listen.

Bottom Line: You community partner will have a story to tell after they have been in your classroom. You want to ensure it is a good one.

Where to Start

So, how do you start connecting with community partners? Large institutions like children's museums and zoos typically have an education department that is seeking partners. When you contact education departments, they already have avenues created to assist your classroom. To solidify this partnership, you want to look for win-win scenarios. How can what you are doing in your class also help them reach their larger goals? More established museums are one of the only places I recommend a cold call, primarily because the folks in the education department are waiting for you to call or are actively seeking educators.

Another place to start is with local, small nonprofits. Executive directors want to tell people about their passion and their cause. The typical executive director of small nonprofits is available during the workday, and their main job is advocacy. If you can help them solve a problem, they will gladly work with you. Nonprofit relationships can be a tremendous win-win scenario and are also a great avenue to teach your learners about giving back to the community.

Before you start spending too much time cold-calling every large business in your area, note that you probably have authentic audiences already in your school district. Older learners love to present to younger learners and often you can find standards that align vertically. There are school board members, principals, and superintendents who can come in, and this can be a great way to garner support for the great things you are doing in your classroom. Parents of learners are other good warm contacts who are right in your district. A simple form sent home could turn up some leads for community partners.

Once you see the benefit to your learning environment, you will begin to pick up community partners everywhere you go.

Resources

All resources listed can be found at: www.magnifylearningin.org/pbl-simplified-book-resources.

- Community Partners
  - Community Partner Guide

Questions

- When did you have a community partner come into your classroom? How did your learners respond?
- Who are some community partners who are already connected to your school?
- What businesses are in your community?
- What nonprofits are in your community?
- What local or state government agencies could you work with?
- What state or community colleges could you partner with?

CHAPTER 9

Norms and Protocols

*"It's hard to be fully creative
without structure and constraint."*
~ David Allen

Norms and protocols give facilitators and learners a framework for learning. Without structure, you can't expect learners or facilitators to know the implied rules. The research of John Hattie shows that one of the top indicators of moving the needle on learning is clarity.[5] We can make the learning environment clear for our learners by using consistent norms and protocols. Facilitators and learners alike operate better within a structure.

Norms are an agreed-upon set of terms that help learning happen in a classroom. Norms should be more than rules, though. Norms should be empowering and should be created through the voice and choice of the learners. There is a big difference between,

"Let's read over the rules of my classroom" and "Now we are going to establish norms that we will all abide by to help make this the best possible learning environment." An established set of norms allows learners a voice in the process of creating structure.

Establishing Norms

Here's a process for setting up norms that you can use in your classroom:

Set-up

- Give every learner post-it notes
- Have a board ready to place all the learner post-it notes on

Action

- Tell learners, "We are going to be establishing norms within our classroom. Norms are the things we consider normal in Room 239, which means we will all live by them the best we can. What do you need to learn best in Room 239?"
- "Please take a stack of post-it notes and write down three things you need to be successful in this class. Write one idea per post-it note. Are there any clarifying questions before we start writing down ideas to make you successful in this class? I'll give you four minutes. Ready? Go!"
- "Let's take another two minutes to write down any more ideas you may have."
- "Next, you will bring your post-it notes up to the front and place them on the board. As you place your post-it notes on the board, read the other ideas and see if they are like yours. If you have a similar idea, place your post-it notes close together. We are going to do this next step without talking.

Any clarifying questions? Can someone please restate in their own words what we are doing in our next step?"

- You will now have your learners up and moving around, placing and reading the norms on the board. You will likely need to do some more directing to help them get their ideas together.

- [Variation] If that sounds like a lot of your learners up and moving, you could put them in smaller groups of three to five learners to help them sort through their norms initially. Then one representative from each group can bring their consolidated norms to the front.

- As the learners are putting their norms on the board, you may want to stop them when you see a positive example. "Ah! Perfect! I see that Caleb put his post-it note about needing quiet time to work next to Sadie's post-it note about needing time to get started on an assignment right away. Good job joining similar ideas!"

- After seven minutes or so, the work will be nearing completion, so thank the learners for their input on forming norms.

- As you look at the board, you will see some natural groupings. Work to create categories for each grouping. As you create a category, ask the learners, "Does this wording capture what you were thinking?"

- As you thank the learners for their work in creating a collaborative classroom environment where all learners can be heard and can thrive, continue to remind them these norms have come from them and everyone will work to live by them.

- If something is obviously absent, you might say, "Do we need anything about protecting everyone's voice?" to fill in the gap the learners may have missed.

Typically, you end up with a list that does look much like the rules you typically create and hand out, but there is a difference for the learners. The learners have now been involved in the process of creating norms. This empowering step makes a big difference to a classroom culture and is well worth the twenty minutes of class time. As you correct classroom behavior, you can point to the class-created norms instead of your rules. It is not you against the class enforcing your unfair rules. It is you helping enforce the wishes and needs of their fellow classmates. If you want to add another level, you can have everyone sign the norms, saying they agree to abide by them. You may need to hold a "How to Sign Your Name" workshop to do this, which is also very valuable learning.

"Education is not the filling of a pail, but the lighting of a fire."
~ William Butler Yeats

Living by Norms

Congratulations! You have given up some of your control to the learners by allowing them to help set up your classroom norms. Now it is time to model living out these norms. I suggest pointing out every time you do something because of the norms for at least the first couple of weeks. It may sound like, "Since I have presented new information, I am going to give you some individual work time. Norm #6 states you would like some time to process individually after new information is presented." It can be even better if you find you have missed a norm, "Whoa! I apologize. I just realized (or Luke pointed out) that I have not upheld one of our norms. Norm #2 states we will provide some quick study time before a test. Let's take five minutes to let you review your notes." Show the learners you are human and it is acceptable to miss a norm. Just be sure to apologize and get back on track.

If one learner has a problem with another learner, you may ask, "Which of our norms do you feel was not upheld?" Or a learner may come to you and say, "Mr. Steuer, you are not following norm #3." In any case, it is essential for you to be open and professional when demonstrating and upholding norms, and it is empowering to give learners a voice in establishing a classroom culture.

Protocols

Protocols are a tool for bringing organization and direction to conversations so that all voices have an opportunity to be heard. Protocols provide necessary support for collaboration, feedback, and clarity for Project Based Learning work to happen. Ultimately, protocols are another powerful culture-building piece for your classroom as structures designed to increase collaboration, efficiency, and professionalism. Learners and facilitators alike appreciate the organization that comes with a protocol because everyone knows the rules and their roles and realizes their voices will be heard. A protocol is used to protect the voice of the introvert and focus the voice of the extrovert. As we honor the rules of protocols, we show learners that they don't have to be the loudest to be heard.

 "Protocols are a tool for bringing organization and direction to conversations so that all voices have an opportunity to be heard." ~ Ryan Steuer

After running a protocol for the first time, I suggest a debrief period to see how well it was received. A debrief period allows your learners a moment to reflect on the learning that just occurred. As noted in Chapter 7, reflection shouldn't just be at the end of a PBL Unit. We want to reflect and adjust as we go through the PBL process. Reflecting and adjusting is a way to give our learners more voice and choice. We are asking them, "How did this protocol work for you?" When they say it worked well, we say, "Great, we will do more of these since they are helping you learn." If they have some cool feedback, we say, "Thank you for engaging in this protocol and for giving your feedback. What adjustments do you suggest for next time?" Either way, we are honoring the learner's voice, empowering them to give feedback, and showing them their voice is important, which encourages them to use their voice more in appropriate ways.

Win Story

Using a modified Tuning Protocol, as adults, we often tune PBL project ideas. Each time we address "likes," "wonders," and next steps, a previously stuck facilitator says, "Thank you! The group has helped solve my main obstacle. Now I have a lot of ideas to help me going forward." This has happened over and over again. A quick, eight-minute Tuning Protocol uses the expertise of the group to solve a problem and serves as an excellent lesson for facilitators and learners: the smartest person in the room *is* the room.

 "The smartest person in the room, is the room."
~ David Weinberger

Fail Story

When running a protocol called Connections with my learners for the first time, I used a timeframe I typically used for adults. This extended timeframe allowed for a full three minutes of silence at the end of each round. Excited about running a protocol and teaching my learners the value of silence, we all waited. While I very much believe in the importance of teaching learners the value of silence, three minutes of awkwardly looking at each other was a bit much! After reflecting on the protocol as a group, we decided we weren't ready to tackle the extended length of time yet. Based on the learner feedback, we changed the timeframes and saw great success, and we eventually worked our way up to extended times. We don't have to be afraid of these fail stories because they can be turned into authentic, transparent learning experiences for us and the learners.

Bottom Line: Norms and protocols give everyone a voice and a safe, organized structure for learning.

Where to Start

How do you jump in with a practical set of norms using protocols? Jump in with one class and set up norms via the action steps in this chapter. Sometimes it's overwhelming to think about starting something new with *all* our learners. Even if you are reading this in the middle of the year, go ahead and run the norms protocol. Learners love to give their voice, and you will get a small taste of running your first protocol. If you are already accustomed to protocols, check out the resources for this chapter for a list of protocols that work well in a PBL classroom.

Resources

All resources listed can be found at: www.magnifylearningin.org/pbl-simplified-book-resources.

• Protocols

- *PBL Simplified* Video Series—Protocols
- Protocol Video Series
  - I guide your whole staff through a series of protocols.

Questions

- Do you speak up during staff meetings? Why or why not?
- Would a protocol help you and others share their thoughts?
- Learners have different learning and sharing preferences. When have you been successful at meeting an individual learner's unique needs?

CHAPTER 10

Voice and Choice

"If you deny people their own voice,
you'll have no idea of who they were."
~ Alice Walker

Voice and choice empower learners as they participate in the process of learning. Instead of school just being something that happens *to* learners, we invite them to participate through voice and choice. School is an unavoidable reality for learners, and when they finally get some choice in how they learn, it empowers them. Passive or apathetic learners can become active learners when they are a part of the decision-making process.

When you give any person choice, they have the opportunity to step up and participate. In a meta-analysis study examining the effect of choice on intrinsic motivation, "Results indicated that providing choice enhanced intrinsic motivation, effort, task performance, and perceived competence, among other outcomes."[6] Do you want your learners to increase their effort and better their task performance? Of course; however, I wouldn't be surprised if the idea of giving learners voice and choice scares you. Giving your learners voice and choice is brave work, but the journey is worth it for you and your learners.

I meet with many teachers who are ready to give all their classroom decisions to the learners, and I meet with teachers who never give learners choice because the one time they gave them choice, it did not go well. So, I've learned to explain voice and choice as a continuum. On the left side, you have a teacher-dominated choice structure. Moving toward the right side, you start giving choice about which pencils learners can use, then you let them choose their seats, their group members, etc. If you keep going far enough to the right, you have anarchy! Anarchy in the classroom is not good at any level.

Teacher guidance for every decision creates passivity, and while anarchy is likely very engaging, it's not great for productive learning and collaborating. Neither end of the spectrum is great, so you must find your sweet spot in the middle. This sweet spot may depend on the age and maturity of the learners, your experience and learning curve with voice and choice, and the specific project.

Implementing voice and choice falls under a growth mindset because you want to continually improve and make your way toward the right side of the spectrum to the level that's appropriate for you and your learners. If you hit anarchy, just pull back a bit!

Voice and choice get lumped together when we talk about empowering learners, which makes sense because they are similar

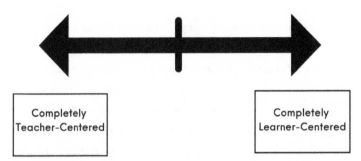

concepts, but here I define each separately and provide some examples of how to get started.

Voice

The opposite of Alice Walker's quote at the beginning of the chapter is: *If you **give** people their own voice, you'll **have** an idea of who they were.* Giving learners voice is allowing them to be heard.

Contrary to the thought that may have popped up in the back of your mind, voice does not mean that learners always get what they want. There are many ways to integrate voice into your classroom that get your learners to lean into the work. A small step might be to ask them for feedback on a PBL Unit or activity that you have just completed (as discussed in Chapter 6). After you finish an activity, you can ask your learners two questions:

- What did you like about this activity?
- What would you change about this activity if we did it again?

You could put these questions at the end of your unit exam, or you could use post-it notes to make it an Exit Ticket. However you collect the information, it is important that you ask the question and that everyone gets to participate. When you ask, you are telling learners that their voice matters in your classroom. You are telling them that as they engage in your classroom, they can make a difference.

Another example of integrating voice into your classroom culture is through a learner voice group that meets monthly or weekly. These sessions can be a time to get feedback on how projects are going or how the culture is forming. While learner voice groups should not be an avenue for learners to get whatever they want, they should be shown some early wins to let them know we are listening. As an example, a learner voice group may determine that there should be a new vending machine, more bathroom breaks, time to listen to music, and more structured work time. A facilitator may point out in the next week when they give an additional bathroom break that this extra time was incorporated based on feedback from the learner voice group. They might also talk with the voice group about the cost involved with and school rules about bringing in a new vending machine. The learner voice group is meant to create a space for conversation, so it may also be a time for the facilitator to bring up some concerns they have about the way some things are progressing in the classroom to get feedback. Voice is allowing learners to be heard in an environment that has typically asked them to sit down, be quiet, and comply.

A learner voice group does not have to be super structured to get started and is a great way to dip your toe a little deeper into learner voice. Invite a group of seven to ten learners into your classroom for lunch once a month. Choose a variety of learners, so you can hear their diverse viewpoints. You will likely find your learners are more likely to talk in this setting than the normal classroom setting. Have a few questions ready ahead of time and be ready to take notes. Taking notes is a good body language signal for your learners that tells them what is being said is important to you. As you practice, you will begin to hone your listening skills and your ability to provide voice to your learners.

"The one thing that you have that nobody else has is you. Your voice, your mind, your story, your vision. So write and draw and build and play and dance and live as only you can."
~ Neil Gaiman

Learner voice teams are a win. Even if they are not perfect to start, giving learners an outlet in which to speak their minds is always a good idea for building a culture of invested learners.

To get started with a learning voice team of your own, nothing will help you learn like jumping in and gaining experience, but here are a few suggestions:

- Make the learning voice team a diverse subset of your learners
- Make it public
- Rotate learners on and off the learning voice team
- Ask their opinions . . . take some of them
- Meet regularly
- Tell learners not currently on the learning voice team to talk with someone who is if they have an idea or concern

Choice

Giving learners choice is giving learners some control over their learning. Again, historically, education has been about control and compliance, so when we give learners even the smallest amount of choice, they respond enthusiastically. We may not be ready to give learners a choice in which standards they want to engage, but we can offer a choice in which pathways they take to show mastery of the standards. There are still non-negotiables, but we need to identify the aspects of education that are negotiable and give these choices to learners as often as we can. Choice starts to build some autonomy, which research shows creates engagement.[7]

An example of a choice you may start with could be a Choice Board. A Choice Board can be simple or elaborate, but you want to give the learners multiple ways to prove their learning. Googling Choice Boards will give you a variety of creative options to model after. As you find out what works best for your learners, you will strike a balance of rigor and engagement that allows your learners choice and you a way to prove they have mastered a set of standards. Start small and grow!

Win Story

Have you ever had the 1 p.m. lunch spot? We all know that every innovative, educational initiative is really run by the bus and lunch schedules. If you get the first lunch spot, you may be eating a brunch, but the last slot feels like a forced fast. The learner voice team pointed out the obvious—this is not awesome. Without a learner voice team, learners are just complaining daily, but with a learner voice team, we can lend a compassionate ear and look for possible learner-created solutions.

While discussing the last-lunch-period conundrum, the challenge put back to the learning voice team was to come up with a solution instead of just complaining. The final proposed solution was a vending machine. While a vending machine seems like an easy solution, the current vending machine only offered candy, which was not really a solution to hunger or nutrition. After some lively discussion, the learning voice team came up with a solution of selling more nutritious snacks during a set time between periods with the proceeds going to fund team activities. With some additional work—and reasonable parameters—the facilitators agreed to allow nutritious snacks, and the learning voice team gained a big win. From that point on, facilitators could ask, "Do you remember when we listened and put in the snack passing period?" Learners saw facilitators open the communication channels, which built a trust that empowered the learners.

"I'm not afraid of confrontation. It doesn't have to be an argument. We all have a voice. And they are all worth listening to."
~ Adam Goodes

Fail Story

Seeing how choice and autonomy empower learners, we set up a system of workshop rotations learners could choose from.

Me: "Anna, did you go to my complex sentence workshop?"

Sara: "No."

Me: "Why not?"

Sara: "You told us to choose our schedules. I didn't pick that one."

Me: "But don't you need help with complex sentences?"

> **Sara:** "I guess, but it didn't sound cooler than the tech work-shop or the team-building workshop. Maybe you should have a more engaging title like you are always telling us."

And through the seemingly sound logic of an eighth grader, mandatory workshops were born! Choice is great, but sometimes kids don't pick what is best for them. Data-based Need to Knows provide a systematic way of assigning mandatory workshops. I also want to point out here that while we want to move along the spectrum of voice and choice, we do still hold the right to assign workshops or assignments when needed.

Bottom Line: Voice and choice will empower learners to be active participants in their learning.

Where to Start

Remember, voice and choice is a continuum, so where you start is up to you and your learners. To increase the voice in your classroom, you may add a couple of reflective questions at the end of your unit, such as: "What did you like about this unit? What would you change for next year's class?" As you start to see the power of learner voice, you may want to have a group come in during lunch to talk with you. Adding choice to your classroom can start small as well. You may start by giving them a choice of how the desks are arranged or which medium they would like to use to prove mastery of the standards, or simply asking them what they need to learn. As you begin to build voice and choice into your classroom culture, you will see learners begin to advocate for their learning. Once learners know you will listen to them, they will tell you the best way they learn or if they need a workshop again. When you start on this journey of voice and choice, you will have some hiccups, but you won't ever turn back.

Resources

All resources listed can be found at:
www.magnifylearningin.org/pbl-simplified-book-resources.

- Voice and Choice
  - Student Voice and Choice Tips

Questions

- Are you still uncomfortable giving up some control in your classroom?
- What is one baby step you can take toward voice and choice?
- What is one deeper level of choice you can give your learners?
- Where are you already giving your learners voice and choice?
- How can you help gather your learners' voices?

CHAPTER 11

Grading

"Grades improve learning only when accompanied by specific guidance and direction from teachers on how to improve. A score and grade at the top of a paper does nothing to help students improve."
~ Thomas Guskey

What does the grade of a "C" mean in your class? Does it mean a learner mastered the content but didn't do the homework? Does it mean a learner turns in assignments late? Does it say a learner knows very little about the content but is compliant and turns things in? If you have never looked at your grading closely, know that it likely can mean many of those things. When we jump into Project Based Learning, we also assess learners' Employability Skills. While adding non-standard-based content to our grades is gaining acceptance, we still want to make sure we know exactly what our grades mean. The letter grade we give is only one communication tool we have at our disposal, but it has been given a lot of emphasis, so we should make sure we know what we are communicating. This chapter provides practical tips that push your thinking to figure out how to grade what is most important for your learners.

Of course, you need to grade things you think are important. Content mastery, work ethic, collaboration, and participation are all important. So, how do we grade these important ideas? And how do we communicate the grading of these in a way that allows learners to see progress?

To communicate openly about your grades, it helps to separate your grade into buckets. Even though PBL pushes you to infuse Employability Skills into your classrooms and gradebook, I realize you were hired to teach a specific content area. To this end, a large bucket of your grade should be your content area. When you give a test directly related to your standards, those points should go into your content bucket; however, if you are going to communicate clearly about your grading, you cannot decrease a grade in the content bucket if a learner turns in an assignment late.

Before you close this book thinking anarchy is going to set in, know that you can still give or take away points for turning in late work to help communicate expectations, but let's create another bucket to capture that. What if you create a work ethic grading bucket? A learner may have mastered genetics, but they are not well organized, so they turn in all their work a week late. This learner would receive an "A" for their content work and an "F" (or "needs improvement") for their work ethic.

Are you beginning to see how grading buckets can help clearly communicate expectations?

Inevitably, grading group work comes up any time we hold a Project Based Learning workshop over the summer. Group work has historically been disdained by learners, parents, and even teachers—and for good reason. In a typical setting, one learner does all the work, but everyone gets the same grade, or one group member lets people down, and everyone's grade suffers. So, how can we effectively teach our learners collaboration and make sure their grade is earned by them—not the overall group?

If we use the bucket method, we can separate content, work ethic, collaboration, and presentation grades. This provides a distinct advantage over traditional group work. For example, you can create standards-based assessments that show a learner's individual mastery. If you allow that individual content grade to make up 85 percent of a learner's grade, it ensures that the majority of their grade is earned by them in your content area. Then the other 15 percent of their grade can be 5 percent work ethic, 5 percent presentation, and 5 percent collaboration.

- 85 percent = Content
- 5 percent = Work ethic
- 5 percent = Presentation
- 5 percent = Collaboration

This balance of buckets allows group work to still be assessed, so we can give feedback, but not so heavily that it overpowers the content grade. Essentially, with this proposed balance, a learner can actively be in a group and still earn 95 percent of their grade on their own. We have beaten back the idea that a bad group can ruin a learner's grade.

This is just one example of how a grade can be communicated. As educators, we need to be able to explain our grade breakdown to our parents and learners. Can you effectively explain why a learner has a particular grade in your class? Studying a book about grading is a worthy endeavor and will leave you more confident in your teaching practice moving forward. See the resources section at the end of this chapter for suggestions.

"Students can learn without grades, but they can't learn without timely, descriptive, feedback."
~ Rick Wormelli

Win Story

When you grade Employability Skills, you see learners display them. We want our learners to present well; we want to teach them the skills they will need in college and/or the workforce. In elementary schools practicing Employability Skills, you can tour and hear from a panel of learners who will masterfully answer your questions. I experienced this when I attended an expo of learning. I was greeted by a nine-year-old, articulate tour guide (they must have practiced their tour guide responsibilities!) and blown away by the panel's answers. The learners on the panel were prepared and showed obvious learning. They were not reading from notecards and were taking impromptu questions from the adults in the audience.

After the panel discussion concluded, I was asked a profound question that entrenched me more into this work, "Which of those learners do you think has an Individualized Education Program (IEP)?" I realized it was nearly impossible to tell. I would have been making a total guess. PBL for these learners had erased the normal lines between the kids who are good at the game of school and those who may struggle. All the kids shone with confidence and were eager to share their learning.

Fail Story #1

We got to the end of one project and our learners had done nothing. I created a great project that was authentic and engaging. We let the learners work in groups so that they could produce even more work. A couple of days before they were going to present, we had practice presentations. I asked the first group to present, and they were miserably underprepared. The same thing happened with the next three groups. I stopped everyone after that and used the rest of the day to meet with groups, so they could get where they needed to be.

My big mistake was waiting until the end of the project to assign a grade. The majority of their grade was going to be wrapped up in a five-minute presentation. I realized we needed benchmark grades for learners to grow into their presentations and projects, and I needed to be able to see where learners were in their learning to help them move forward. After that experience, I advocated for many benchmarks in Step 3 of the PBL process before the presentation with the presentation being more of an authentic celebration of the learning instead of a frantic and futile race for us to assign grades.

Fail Story #2

I've asked Andrew Larson, who shared his big yeast-discovering win in Chapter 3, to share a Fail Story here. I've placed Andrew's Fail Story here in the grading chapter because his grading "commandment" will serve you well as you continue your PBL journey. Also note, Andrew learned from the failure and sought help.

The biggest fail I can remember came with my very first PBL project. It was 2008, and the course was (and still is) called Global Science Perspectives. It is an integration of English 9 and Environmental Stud-

ies. To this day, I feel that this course is one of my proudest accomplishments, despite the reality that it has occasionally been bumpy, vague, disorganized, messy, overstuffed, undersized, and overenrolled.

We had opened our school just a month prior and we had all kinds of bizarre ideas about what we should be doing (and what our kids should be doing). I am happy to report that there is a lot that I do not remember about the details of the project; in retrospect, that is probably because we had no idea what we were actually doing.

We were building a course from scratch. It was somewhat like "building a plane whilst flying the plane." I remember being super excited about what we were creating and arrogantly assuming that it was going to be inherently great. I had read a bit about the constructivist nature of Project Based Learning and got the misplaced idea that in PBL, learners were largely in charge of teaching themselves stuff. And since we didn't really know what our course was going to be about, we thought it would be apt to take a . . . Constructivist approach . . . to this first project.

My co-facilitator and I asked our learners to design a cover for a yet-to-be published curriculum guide for a course that we were creating in real time, for the first time. (Does this sound like a setup for failure?) The concept (cough) was to help learners understand what the course was really about. The problem was that we were still figuring that out for ourselves.

The night before the presentations, I got a call from an agitated parent. She was advocating for her daughter, who didn't understand what she was supposed to present and was distraught. I was groggy with sleep and didn't give a very good response to the mother's concerns. When it came time for this learner's group to give their presentation, the gloves came off. Instead of presenting on the assigned content, this learner (who, I might add, was one of our very best) delivered a pointed *rebuke by analyzing the breakdown in her group's collaboration. The conclusion was that their group had failed because we (her instructors) had failed to teach them how to collaborate. Never have I wanted to disappear below my desk as much as during this presentation.*

You could say there were a minimum of two big red flags in this project concept. The first, and biggest, was a lack of clarity of goals and a content-driven, standards-based approach on our part. I mean, okay, we knew that we wanted learners to design a cover that would reflect a series of global themes in some artistic and visually intriguing way. Clearly, then, we had to introduce them to these enormous global abstractions like climate change, poverty, food inequity, religious strife, and more. There was no way that we could realistically give them a "glossy overview" of these topics in a way that was meaningful. In this way one could say that it lacked a focus on content. And THAT is a major issue. "I just don't feel like I'm learning anything," one learner said quite memorably.

"You just have to trust the process," we replied. That's reasonable advice from an educator to a learner . . . so long as the educators do, in fact, have a, uh, process, in place.

The other major issue, and one that I've devoted a lot of time to in writing and in communication with other educators, is based on a "commandment" of sorts that one cannot assess that which one does not teach. In our case, we did not teach. In the PBL classroom, there are a myriad of different skill sets coming into play, from cognitive processes around content to interpersonal communication and development of social skills. There really is too much going on to possibly track. That's fine, so long as the one in charge doesn't decide that every subset of learner performance needs to be measured. I mean, they could measure it all, but only if it all falls into the caveat that it's been purposefully taught to kids, and not just once, but repeatedly, and in real ways that mimic the assessment format. As I have gained experience in facilitation of PBL, I have grown far more comfortable with very small and incremental progress made by learners over years, not weeks. Additionally, the steps are more concrete, not less. Learners completing a group contract together is evidence of collaboration. Using said group contract to make decisions and resolve conflict is a bit more advanced and takes more time and experience to grasp and master. Baby steps.

The silver lining of this situation is that as a result of this feedback, we sought some professional help and brought in a high-functioning executive team from Cummins, Inc., our local Fortune 500 company. In what became a weeks-long tutorial and series of demonstrations, they showed us how it should look when people work together on common goals. Failure, and an early one at that, proved to be a valuable teacher . . . as it often is.

Bottom Line: You get what you grade, and you can only grade what you teach; therefore, if you want learners who have Employability Skills like collaboration, problem-solving, creativity, and grit, you must explicitly teach and grade these skills.

Where to Start

Ask yourself what it means to get an "A," "C," or "F" in your class. Look at some examples by picking names out of your gradebook. Write three names down and then a small bullet point narrative of why they have their assigned grade. Do you have some learners with "A"s who are compliant and kind but really don't know the content? If a learner received a "C" or "F" from you, is it because they failed your tests or because they didn't turn in their assignments? When I first did this exercise, I realized I had learners who knew more content than their grade showed. The zeroes I put in the gradebook for homework assignments masked the content they had mastered.

Here are more reflective grading questions:

- What do you think your grade should represent?
- If a learner turned everything in and participated in discussions but failed all your tests, what grade would they get?
- If a learner didn't turn in any work but aced all your tests, what grade would they receive?

As a next step, ask a colleague to engage in these questions with you. Dig into and try to challenge some of your beliefs around grading. This conversation is already happening in schools, so see what others are saying. Type in "why you shouldn't give zeroes as grades" to Google and see where this takes you. Don't be afraid of the discussion. It will only lead to more intentional work for you and your learners.

Resources

All resources listed can be found at:

https://www.magnifylearningin.org/pbl-simplified-book-resources

- *What We Know About Grading* by Thomas R. Guskey and Susan M. Brookhart
- Rubrics and Assessments

Questions

- Name a learner who has received an "A" in your class. Name another who has received a "C" in your class. Name another learner who has received an "F" in your class.

- Why did they receive these grades?
- Did they master the content? Did they do extra credit? Did they know the content but have missing assignments? Did they have a zero in your gradebook?

CHAPTER 12

School Implementation

"It's important to have a sound idea, but the really important thing is the implementation."
~ Wilbur Ross

"**R**yan, I get that Project Based Learning is awesome for facilitators and learners. Now how do I get PBL started at my school?"

I have gotten some form of this question nearly every day for the last decade. I've been doing this long enough now to know that I can't just dive into answering that question without participating in folly. When educators ask me this question today, I ask them to tell me about their situation. To save you some time if you choose to reach out to me (And I hope you do!), below is a list of questions I will end up asking during our conversation.

1. Have you developed a compelling "why" for moving to Project Based Learning?
2. Will you have grade-level PBLs or individual classroom PBLs?
3. How will you communicate this move to PBL to your stakeholders (e.g., teachers, learners, parents, community)?
4. How will you support PBL-trained teachers?
5. How will you support untrained teachers?
6. How will you make the work public?
7. How will you change your building's professional development?
8. What does your three-year plan look like?
   - Training and support
   - Vision Document

These questions get you to start thinking about your context. Where you start depends on your context, so before you read through the four implementation models and each of their benefits and cautions, I want you to intentionally think about your context. It helps to make this a collaborative section of the book, so invite your colleagues to dream with you. The more stakeholders you get involved in the change process, the better chance you have of success. There is no one perfect implementation model, so you will need to read with the intent to figure out which model best fits your context. While all of these implementation models have produced positive results, I do recommend Learning Teams, so I give it more text and a guest contributor.

Below are the four models to implement Project Based Learning at your school:

1. School Within a School
2. Whole School Implementation

3. Separate School
4. Learning Teams

School Within a School

A School Within a School implementation model is often implemented in the secondary levels. For example, you may teach at a middle or high school with over one thousand learners, and you create a Project Based Learning wing with 25 percent of those learners who will engage their standards through Project Based Learning. The learners in this new wing are typically chosen through a stratified lottery that ensures the population of the new wing has the same makeup of learners as the other parts of the building.

All learners still have access to the same special classes, sports, band, and choir. Classes in the Project Based Learning wing may look different, but they often still use the same common assessments as the traditional classrooms in the building. School Within a School models allow districts to have a K–12 PBL track for learners without having to completely convert their middle and high schools to Project Based Learning.

Benefits

- Uses a lot of the same resources already in place
- The work is public for other staff and learners to see
- Measuring success is easy because there are a lot of variables that stay the same. Results of the School Within a School and the rest of the building are easy to gather
- Learners have access to the same specials and extracurricular opportunities

Cautions

- Can create division between staff and learners from different wings of the building (Us versus Them)
- Professional development should be differentiated for different parts of the building

Whole School Implementation

A Whole School Implementation is pretty self-explanatory. Existing schools decide they are going to fully adopt Project Based Learning as their instructional model and begin training. The district, principal, teachers, and parents share a vision for what a PBL school could look like, and they set out on the PBL journey together.

Communication is often the key to this implementation strategy, so stakeholders have similar expectations. In all these implementation strategies, you are engaging in the change process. People inherently resist change, even if it is for the better, so we need to include stakeholders as we bring Project Based Learning to our communities. Bring stakeholders to early school visits and visioning meetings. Early inclusion to the process will help you build outside advocates for your work.

Benefits

- Clear, consistent vision
- Training of teachers is consistent and opens itself to mentoring opportunities
- Building culture can be consistent and synergistic across the whole building

Cautions

- Not all staff may be on board with a change

- Community members and parents may be accustomed to school being like it was when they grew up

"Implementation of promises is as important as making them."
~ Y. S. Jaganmohan Reddy

Separate School

Separate School is another easy one to explain. This is when a district opens a new school with a Project Based Learning focus. Everyone enrolling in this school realizes they will be engaging in learning differently, and they know why. A separate high school option often makes sense with this implementation model. Start with a group of learners who see the benefits of a different instructional model.

Districts sometimes open a separate PBL school as a place to address a local business or industry need. As local industry asks for an employee base that has more Employability Skills, a district or community may agree to create an education option where learners are specifically focusing on Employability Skills through PBL. Medical, automotive, electrical, welding, or other trades may also drive a separate school with a Project Based Learning focus.

A separate PBL school can also start on the elementary end of a district to start PBL moving through a district. As the learners begin learning in a new, more engaged manner, the learners and parents can be active stakeholders in helping to create momentum for PBL in higher grades.

Benefits
- Culture can be easier to create
- Communication of the culture can be easier

- Teachers and learners who step up to attend are excited to join the movement

Cautions

- Can sometimes be seen as an alternative school if not communicated clearly
- Can become separated from the rest of the district

Learning Teams

If you ask me which implementation model has the most opportunity for success, I lean heavily toward Learning Teams. To help give you an overview of the process, I asked Jeff Spencer to add some words of wisdom. Jeff has implemented PBL several times in different schools with success in every category you can think of, from standardized tests to learner empowerment.

While Jeff Spencer is now serving his district from a central office position, he was the principal at Southport Elementary School in Indianapolis, Indiana, a Title I Distinguished School and TAP Founder's Award winner. Jeff was also the principal at Washington Discovery Academy, the first New Tech Network Elementary Demonstration Site. Prior to moving to administration, Jeff taught seventh- and eighth-grade social studies. Because seventh and eighth graders don't typically care about social studies, Jeff quickly moved to PBL as an instructional model and has never looked back.

Change process and leading successful implementation of Project Based Learning requires staff buy-in, leadership support, and a shift in structures and process. Before I jump into those concepts in more depth, I want to share my story and the reason Project Based Learning has been my guiding light as an educator.

PBL has been my personal passion for over a decade. I have been a facilitator, instructional coach, administrator, and even a parent in a PBL environment. From early implementation, PBL provided a "why" and relevancy for my learners, and I have been a passionate advocate and implementer ever since. After fourteen years in Decatur Township located in Indianapolis, Indiana, I took a risk and moved my family and professional career to Plymouth, Indiana to serve as the principal at Washington Discovery Academy (WDA), a K–4 New Tech Network PBL elementary school.

I had admired Plymouth from afar as they committed to a K–12 PBL implementation and was excited to join the team. WDA is an exceptional school, and we were recognized as the first elementary school New Tech Network Demonstration Site and also won the Best in Network Award for the best project in the entire New Tech Network while I worked there. I strongly suggest a visit if you are thinking about PBL. While I grew and learned so much, Plymouth was too far away from home and Indianapolis, so we moved back after two years in Northern Indiana.

I was fortunate to be selected to serve as principal of Southport Elementary School (SES) in Perry Township. SES was another outstanding place of learning, nationally recognized as a Title I Distinguished School, and was also a recipient of the Founders Awards from the National Institute for Excellence in Teaching. The staff was incredible, and while I wasn't hired specifically to integrate PBL, it became a natural fit.

Perry Township used NIET's Best Practice rubric, and embedded into the expectations of daily lessons are aspects like motivating learners with content that is personally engaging and relevant to learners and lessons that build inquiry, curiosity, and exploration. There are also high-level indicators that focus on getting learners to ask questions and then attempt to answer them, give high quality feedback to peers, and think practically by applying their learning to use and implement what they learn in real-life scenarios. Sounds a lot like PBL, right? Our staff was at a high-functioning school seeking what could push them to the next level. I left Plymouth thinking my PBL journey might be done but found a perfect place for another PBL implementation.

As you lead change, it is important to think about those key ideas from earlier: staff buy-in, leadership support, and a shift in structures and process. There would be no PBL training before my first year, but we did have time for key shifts and learning that would support the PBL journey.

Staff Buy-In

Staff buy-in was the first key shift. At our first retreat, we used the Connections Protocol to build culture and introduce protocols in a low-risk environment. We watched Simon Sinek tell us about the power of "why" and allowed teachers to document their reason for being an educator, which hung in our staff lounge throughout the year. Staff members created visuals to identify the traits and characteristics of our ideal graduate, which identified many things that quality PBL created for learners. Our retreat sessions offered staff an opportunity to learn an overview about PBL and challenged them to find a simple way to make learning more relevant. Finally, our weekly adult learning focused our early learning around practical thinking and making learning more relevant for our learners. These early shifts laid a foundation for PBL work and helped get staff excited about the possibilities for our learners.

Over Fall Break, around twenty staff traveled to Plymouth to see PBL in action at Washington Discovery Academy. This visit allowed staff to put concrete examples to theoretical discussion and theory. The staff was challenged to take pictures and videos and create a presenta-

tion for our full staff. We had a critical mass of staff members energized about the journey and presenting their reflections to our entire staff. At this point, there was clear buy-in for PBL as an instructional model at our school.

 "As you lead change, it is important to think about those key ideas: staff buy-in, leadership support, and a shift in structures and process."
~ Jeff Spencer

Leadership Support

As a leadership team, supporting our teachers was a critical aspect of our implementation. Our school is highly successful, and we have a hard-working staff that expects great things for our learners and holds themselves to a very high standard. As leaders, we had to encourage risk and possible failure in an environment that supported but also reflected on those experiences. We also had to build the vision and get people to buy in along the way. We were very transparent from the beginning that this was something we felt was right for the building, but we also acknowledged that it would have to fit into the way we do things and that it was not a mandate. Finally, the support had to allow the early adaptors to flourish.

The support included many different roles and approaches. Our administrative team, administrators and instructional coaches, observed and provided feedback to teachers as they implemented our first project. Our staff is also fortunate in that we have three PBL Certified Educators on staff, which allowed for informal coaching and check-ins for those implementing. Finally, we sent PBL Unit reflections to teaching teams after implementation, so they had meaningful reflection on their work.

Shift in Structures and Processes

At the end of the 2017–2018 school year, key structures and processes were put into place for the next step of our implementation. All staff were invited to apply for the opportunity to be a part of some summer training around PBL. They had to commit to do some virtual learning around PBL and project planning before training, attend a two-day session with Magnify Learning, implement their project during the 2018–2019 school year, and meet monthly as a PBL Learning Team.

Our two-day training focused on deepening our PBL understanding, finishing a refined PBL Unit, crafting an elevator speech about why staff should do PBL, and creating some structures for the year.

The year's implementation had bumps but was an overwhelming success! Our PBL Learning Team created sub-groups to support our team's learning, staff learning, sharing our story with stakeholders, and identifying external checks for quality and recognition. Those teams met throughout the year and created the following outcomes:

- *Critical Friends Groups for PBL Learning Team PBL Units*
- *PBL Newsletter that informed families, community, and staff about PBL implementation*
- *Staff breakfast to inform staff about projects and PBL process*
- *Application and recognition as a IDOE STEM Certified School*
- *Fall and Spring PBL Community Partner Breakfasts*

These systems were key in a successful implementation and also allowed us to "field test" what PBL should look like in our building before we implemented PBL building wide. That next summer, our entire staff went through an on-site training with Magnify Learning with a full implementation scheduled for the 2019–2020 school year.

Our journey is unique because a critical attribute of successful implementation is customization. There are important aspects of PBL, but you have to define those elements in the context of your staff and learners. At the same time, there are key pieces that work in all environments. I challenge you to think about how to bring teachers along in the process, support their work, and build structures and processes for a successful implementation. This was my first time using a Learning Team as a part of the implementation process, and it has been a success for us. We were able to identify what worked and now are poised to replicate it as we bring PBL to all learners in all classrooms.

Benefits
- Ability to collect data from learners within your school so that other teachers can see it working
- Spirit of discovery from the teacher point of view rather than new mandates
- Teacher buy-in is grassroots and authentic

Cautions
- Patience and planning are needed from the administrators
- The initial Learning Team needs to have a positive and rigorous experience since it will define PBL for your building

School Implementation Conclusion
"We were able to identify what worked and now are poised to replicate it as we bring PBL to all learners in all classrooms."

Jeff Spencer's last statement is really the thesis for this chapter. You and your stakeholders must look at what works for your context to determine the best implementation model. Whichever model you are thinking through, ask for help and involve key stakeholders early. Many schools have had successful Project Based Learning implementations that you can learn from. Do not take on this work alone.

Resources

All resources listed can be found at:
www.magnifylearningin.org/pbl-simplified-book-resources.

- Future Protocol
- Vision Document
- Demonstration Sites
- What is PBL?

Questions

- Who are the key stakeholders you need to engage to start planning your PBL implementation process?
- Is there somewhere you can visit to see PBL in action?
- What are you already doing that can help you move toward PBL implementation?

CHAPTER 13

Leadership

*"Leadership is the capacity to translate
vision into reality."*
~ Warren Bennis

When I see leadership rise up and be effective at a Project Based Learning school, that effectiveness is never from just one level of the organization. To make sure we hit all levels of leadership, we look at leadership roles for principals, teachers, and learners in this chapter. Leadership is not a solo sport! I examine leadership from each of those three roles in three categories: change process, teams, and collaboration. When we see principals, teachers, and learners working synergistically through the change process in teams that collaborate well, we see an engaged learning system producing high-quality results.

Principals—Change Process

While principals receive a separate license and some training to be able to handle the legal and curricular aspects of their new role, it is rare that attention is given to the difficulty and importance of the change process. Every principal comes into their new position with a wonderful vision of what school can be, but they quickly find that the process of implementing that vision is very complicated. The stakeholders have a wide variety of views of school, and when you look to move in a new direction, you step into the change process.

Before jumping into the change process required for Project Based Learning, I suggest principals contemplate the following list of questions. These questions are also listed in the previous chapter, but there are a few additions for principals here.

- Will you ask teachers to create grade-level PBLs or individual classroom PBLs?
- How will you communicate this Project Based Learning direction to teachers, learners, parents, and community partners?
- How will you support PBL-trained teachers?
- How will you support untrained teachers?
- How will you make learner work public?
- How will you change your building's professional development?
- Develop a compelling "why" you can share with others.
  - Why should people follow you in this new direction?
  - How will Project Based Learning help your stakeholders have a better future?
- How will you support this PBL initiative over the next three years?

If more than two of these questions are unanswered, you may need some more training, collaborating, and research before you jump in, which is great to realize *before* you start the change process.

Don't be discouraged if you have never considered these questions before. This is a healthy place to be and leads us to the teams needed for principals.

Principals—Teams

Teams are a crucial early addition to the PBL process for a principal to help spread the work and create buy-in for staff. If you haven't already, go back to the previous chapter and read Jeff Spencer's leadership team approach to PBL implementation. You will find teams involved throughout. Trying to bring about change process by yourself is a recipe for failure—and not the good kind.

You might start making an informal team right now as you read this book. Tell a small group of stakeholders that you are doing initial research on Project Based Learning and that it looks promising. Have them read this book as well and then start to bounce ideas off them. Ask them where they foresee possible hurdles and how they can help. When you go through the book study with a small group, you can start to gauge who wants to be on your learning team.

Principals—Collaboration

You will want a local team for your school and district to help you implement PBL, but you should also open up your network to include some other principals who understand the work you are about to undertake. At this point, many principals have their own Win and Fail Stories for implementing PBL. Find these folks, pepper them with questions, and ask for stories. These innovators often enjoy telling stories about how PBL has worked well for them. You'll still need to take these stories and make them fit your context, but you can start to build a network for support, resources, and advice.

At Magnify Learning, we host masterminds for principals. These masterminds intentionally connect like-minded innovators who are looking to push the status quo. Masterminds are filled with principals who understand the loneliness of leadership as you do. The loneliness of leadership occurs when you have visionary ideas you can't share with your staff and your work is so different than your family's and neighbors' that you really can't talk about it with anyone. Masterminds thrive in this arena because the principals in these groups are ready to tackle the big issues, operate at a high level, and create relationships that can save you in a tough spot.

There is an application process to join a mastermind, and not everyone is accepted, which you will appreciate once you are in one. You must be operating at a high level, have a growth mind-set, and be ready to give and receive value. When it comes to the collaboration side of things for principals, you need to find a safe place where you can process big thoughts with people who are at your same level.

"Leadership is having a compelling vision, a comprehensive plan, relentless implementation, and talented people working together."
~ Alan Mulally

Teachers—Change Process

While principals are working to lead the broader stakeholder groups through the change process, teachers must start with them-selves. Even if you are fired up about Project Based Learning here toward the end of the book, you need to realize that you likely were successful in the traditional educational setting through your K–12 years, and college set that in stone for you as *the* way to learn. When I work with teachers across the country, I find it helpful to call this out early, so you can be ready for the change that needs to happen in your mindset. Moving from a teacher-centered classroom, where we dispense knowledge and our learners soak it up, simply doesn't work anymore (if it ever did). We need to be able to give up control in some form and realize that our masterful teaching is not what changes lives. The most well-laid lesson plan is wasted when it doesn't move our learner beyond their current situation, while the smallest opportunity for self-discovery can awaken the curious learner inside every apathetic youth. The learning is more important than the teaching.

A quick example of the importance of learning over teaching is to imagine your best lesson—the one you know learners lean into and are engaged with. Then imagine presenting it on the last day of school. It will still be your best lesson, but we know there won't be a ton of learning from it on the last day of school.

You talking more, assigning more, and grading more will only increase passivity and lead you to burn out. Learners don't need more from you; they need different from you. Be ready for the shift as you take the mindset, process, and resources from this book into your classroom. When you are ready, your learners will be ready.

Teachers—Teams

"Teamwork makes the dream work." I don't know who to give credit to for this one, and my kids may already be tired of hearing it, but it's true. Don't do this alone! Have a team to help encourage you, share ideas with you, and share the workload with you.

When you find a team that is ready to walk with you on your Project Based Learning journey, you will have team members with similar mindsets. Mindset is the key, and it will help you problem-solve any local problem you might have. If you are in an elementary school, you can form grade-level teams or maybe lower elementary and upper elementary teams. At the secondary level, you can mix grade levels and subject areas to form a team. Diversity often helps the problem-solving process, so don't be afraid to form a team that may not normally meet.

Set a regular time to meet each week before or after school, and start your journey together!

Teachers—Collaborate

Look to collaborate with other teachers inside and outside of your school district to gain new perspectives and pick up new tools. Social media can help you find like-minded educators. Those who educate with PBL are still quite receptive to bringing a newbie into their circles to help share their expertise.

Another great way to build your teacher network is to go on a school visit. Take a professional development day to see a PBL school instead of attending a conference. I guarantee you will learn more from a school visit than a conference, and I present at a lot of conferences! Go and see the work being done with learners in the classroom, and then speak with the facilitators during their lunch or prep time. You'll get to ask real-time questions about what you are seeing. Before you leave, make sure you get contact information from the classroom facilitators, so you can follow up to share your wins and ask questions as you start implementing PBL. The facilitators will love sharing their experience with you, and you might be able to bring their classes into one of your PBL Units.

If you need some help finding a school to visit, check out the Magnify Learning list of Demonstration Sites that can be found on our website.

Learners—Change Process

Just as teachers need to rework their mindset, your learners will need time to rework their mindset to address your new expectations of them. Most likely, the learner's expectation up until this point has been some form of "be quiet," "do as I say," "put down on this paper what you think I want," and then learners win with points. This is a very passive stance where learners are always waiting quietly or obstinately for the next thing they are supposed to do to get points. Project Based Learning will be a change they appreciate, but there are some potential mindset roadblocks.

Oddly enough, your high achievers may have the biggest problem initially. Your high achievers have figured out the game of school, know how to get points, and know how to win at school. Winning at school for high achievers looks like getting more points rather than doing more thinking. They have likely already figured out how to best hack your rubric or choice board. But in the long run, they will get PBL and will benefit greatly from the application of the knowledge they have.

If you remember my learner Skyler from Chapter 1, you'll recall he had little to no interest in points. When you note that not turning in an assignment is not good for his grade, he simply doesn't care. Once he discovers that points and grades don't really matter in his world, the apathy only increases. By moving to Project Based Learning and assigning a real "why" to the work, you can increase engagement and get real buy-in from most of your learners, who will see why the change is good for them.

Learners—Teams

We want our learners to work in teams because working in teams comes up on every list of traits employers desire. We want our learners to be successful when they leave our schools, so they need to be able to work in teams. Using the Group Contracts explored in Chapter 5, I have seen learner groups run more smoothly than some state-level teams I'm on! Your learners can do this, and it's good for them. Remember, even if your learners push back on the structure of a Group Contract, they actually want the structure. For any team to work efficiently and peaceably, there needs to be structure.

Once your learners understand how teams can help them, they will be the ones in college who form study groups. They will be the ones in the workplace who are promoted to supervisor. The ability to work on a team is not a natural one, but it is a useful one, and it can be taught. It is worth teaching and modeling!

Learners—Collaborate

Your learners can collaborate even when they are not in formal groups or teams. We want to help our learners interact with diverse subsets of people. When they are in a group chosen at random or they are in a Tuning Protocol, you want them to act professionally to achieve an outcome rather than acting personally offended or responding from emotion. How can your learners learn to interact with a community partner they have never met who may have a very different background than them? Collaboration skills only come from practice in safe and structured learning environments.

This collaboration skill is one of the strongest outcomes of Project Based Learning. By offering your learners many opportunities to do this well—and not so well—until they develop collaboration as a skill, you are giving your learners an enormous leg up in the world. Knowing how to use a compound sentence is nearly useless if you don't know how to talk with people you don't know. A young learner who has spoken to community partners is much more prepared for an interview than one who has not. An applicant may be the best candidate for a job, but if they can't communicate their expertise in a high-pressure situation, they will end up with a lesser job. Ask any employer how their interviews are going, and they will give a negative response. When your learners can look a new person in the eye, shake their hand, and give well-thought-out responses to questions, they will win every time.

***

Leadership in Project Based Learning is about way more than the principal. When we all take a leadership position, Project Based Learning can change lives, schools, and communities. Find a team with the right mindset and begin the conversation today.

"If you could get all the people in the organization rowing in the same direction, you could dominate any industry, in any market, against any competition, at any time."
~ Patrick Lencioni

Win Story

James was a high-achieving point-getter. He knew how school worked and continually won high grades. When we brought in PBL, James had trouble seeing how he would get his points and move on to play basketball. He got his small group, which was self-declared "The Nerd Herd" together to talk with facilitators. They simply didn't see why education needed to change for them, since they were all doing so well with the current status quo.

We listened well and praised them for thinking this through so diligently. We explained again the benefits of PBL and why we were working to apply the concepts we learned in the classroom to the real world. While it took constant messaging for these high achievers, what eventually worked for them was the explanation that our work in school was currently helping people outside of school in many cases. Another big help was the constant message from community partners who mentioned they did not care about grade point averages. Community partners care about collaboration, critical thinking, problem-solving, and the ability to communicate well.

James is a licensed history teacher using Project Based Learning in his classroom. He admits that he wanted the easier path at first, but he has now seen firsthand that Project Based Learning is the best thing for learners.

Fail Story

A thriving PBL School Within a School model that was doing amazing work slowly fizzled after a couple of administrative changes. This grassroots movement had a team of committed teachers pushing the work, but the administrative team was not established enough to handle the change of personnel.

Doing really great work is not enough. We need to be able to create structures, teams, and processes that allow the work to live beyond the talent and personality of a few people. Leadership at all levels is important to the sustainability of this work.

Bottom Line: Nobody does effective Project Based Learning work alone. The work is important enough to get a team together, so start recruiting today.

Where to Start

Wherever you are currently in your Project Based Learning journey, you can start being a leader and create a supportive team. If you have started and are alone in your school doing PBL, recruit a few people who will join you in some way. Reach out to the PBL community to find a collaborator or two. Even if you collaborate from afar via books, podcasts, or YouTube channels, find a trusted source for information and inspiration.

If you are established on your PBL journey, don't forget what got you there. I have seen too many brilliant PBL environments fizzle because one key person leaves and there is no team established. Take a moment to take stock of your leadership equity. Do you have teams supporting the work of the principals, teachers, and learners? If you find one of these areas lacking, start a conversation around making these teams more intentional and stronger.

Resources

All resources listed can be found at:
https://www.magnifylearningin.org/pbl-simplified-book-resources.

- Administrators and Coaches
  - Specific resources for your administrative team
- *PBL Simplified* Book Study
- *PBL Simplified* Podcast
- *PBL Simplified* Video Series

Questions

- Who in your building could be the next member of one of your teams?
- Who could use more support with a team?
- How can you support the next generation of Project Based Learning teachers?
- Where do you have the strongest team?

CONCLUSION

Lifelong Learners

*"The object of education is to prepare the young
to educate themselves throughout their lives."*
~ Robert M. Hutchins

Y ou will not find this book in the self-help section, because you simply cannot do this work on your own. Project Based Learning takes collaborative help to be successful. You can start out as the lone nut (Google "shirtless dancing guy"), but you will need followers and collaborators to help you prob-lem-solve and innovate. And the real key to bringing Project Based Learning to your learners is for you to live the lifestyle yourself. You will need to think critically about things you have always done, revise your work, make your work public, and do all the things you are asking your learners to do. You must be a learner too.

Ultimately, the goal is not for you to be a great teacher but for your learners to become exceptional learners. You may have noticed

I did not use the word "student" in this book. "Student" has a passive connotation. I use the word "learner" because it denotes ongoing action. Your job is to facilitate the awesome. As you step into this new PBL role, you may even stop calling yourself a teacher and switch to the more appropriate descriptor of facilitator.

I will not tell you it is easy; I will simply tell you it is worth it. You didn't say "yes" to this calling to help kids reach average. You committed your life to education to bring opportunities to kids, to show them they are an asset and a gift to the world, and to let every learner know they must share their talents with the world. For learners to see their true capability, they must practice in your classroom. They will not talk to professionals in the real world if we don't give them their first opportunity and show them how. We must model the learning behaviors and hold ourselves to the same high expectations we have of them. We must have unending energy to bring more and more opportunities to kids who otherwise may not have them. Will they take full advantage of every opportunity? Of course not. They are practicing. But when we stick with them, they will find opportunities when it counts, and that is why you entered this profession in the first place. Thank you for your continued dedication to the craft!

Win Story

This book is a compilation of awesome and would not be possible without incredibly awesome facilitators working on the front lines doing amazing things for learners. Share the wins you have on your journey, and don't keep the fails to yourself either. Share it all and move forward. Use your current platform to share the greatness inside your classroom with the world. We can no longer afford for your awesome to stay behind closed doors. Share it and spread it!

Fail Story

The only Fail Story that would be disappointing is if you take no action after reading this book. The goal of *PBL Simplified* is to give you information *and* inspire you to get started on your Project Based Learning journey. You now know the journey will have both wins and fails, but did you pick up the main point? The main point of *PBL Simplified* is: don't wait to be perfect to get started. Start now! Start now, but don't start alone. Know that the wins build on each other, and the wins far outweigh the fails. The fails are merely stepping-stones to more significant wins.

Bottom Line: PBL can change lives. That includes yours!

Where to Start

Learn. Get training. Jump in. Reflect. Repeat times infinity.

Resources

All resources listed can be found at:
https://www.magnifylearningin.org/pbl-simplified-book-resources

- Magnify Learning PBL Workshops
- *PBL Simplified* Book Study
- *7 Steps to Starting PBL*
- What is PBL?

Questions

- What do you need next to move forward on your PBL journey?
  - Information?
  - Inspiration?

- - Action?
  - Training?
- Where can you take a small step forward on your Project Based Learning journey?
- Is there a school you can visit that is already engaging in Project Based learning?

WHAT DID YOU THINK?

First of all, thank you for being on the journey to live out your "why" and make education a great experience for every learner! There are a lot of educational books out there, so thank you for engaging with this book.

I hope it added value to your school and classroom. If it did, would you send a quick message out to your professional learning network (PLN) on Twitter or Facebook to share the PBL love?

If you enjoyed this book and found ways to implement these ideas into your teaching practice, I'd love to hear from you and hope you can take the time to post a review on Amazon or Goodreads. Feedback and reviews fuel this process and keep the movement going!

FURTHER RESOURCES

To connect your entire staff through a book study with discussion/reflection questions and actionable next steps, go to

www.magnifylearningin.org/pbl-simplified-book-resources

for a FREE download. The book study begins engaging adults in the processes and mindsets presented in this book. Without engaging in the material with others and taking action, the concepts found in this book will never change mindsets or behavior. Build culture with a common vocabulary and create a safe space to grow with a supportive peer group working in the same direction.

ABOUT THE AUTHOR

Ryan Steuer launched the first Project Based Learning middle school in the country and is the founder of Magnify Learning, a PBL professional development organization that equips teachers, instructional coaches, and principals across the country to engage learners, tackle boredom, and transform classrooms. Prior to founding Magnify Learning, Ryan was an engineer for a Fortune 50 company, an eighth-grade English teacher, and a missionary. He shares his education and leadership insights on YouTube and on the *PBL Simplified* podcast.

ENDNOTES

1 Remy Dou, Zahra Hazari, Katherine Dabney, Gerhard Sonnert, and Philip Sadler, "Early informal STEM experiences and STEM identity: The importance of talking science," *Science Education* 103, no. 3 (May 2019): 623–637, https://doi.org/10.1002/sce.21499.

2 SHRM, "Employers Say Students Aren't Learning Soft Skills in College," SHRM, published October 21, 2019, https://www.shrm.org/resourcesandtools/hr-topics/employee-relations/pages/employers-say-students-arent-learning-soft-skills-in-college.aspx.

3 Ashley Brooks, "7 Skills Employers Look For Regardless of the Job," Rasmussen University, published September 2019, https://www.rasmussen.edu/student-experience/college-life/skills-employers-look-for/.

4 Mary Lorenz, "1 in 2 Employers Know About a Candidate Within First 5 Minutes," CareerBuilder, published January 2017, https://resources.careerbuilder.com/news-research/1-in-2-employers-know-about-a-candidate-within-first-5-minutes.

5 Cathy Gassenheimer, "Hattie Says Teacher Clarity is One of the Top Learning Interventions. Here's How It Works," A+ Education Partnerships, published October 2019, https://aplusala.org/best-practices-center/2019/10/31/hattie-says-teacher-clarity-is-one-of-top-learning-interventions-heres-how-it-works/.

6 Erika Patall, Harris Cooper, and Jorgianne Civey Robinson, "The Effects of Choice on Intrinsic Motivation and Related Outcomes: A Meta-Analysis of Research Findings," *Psychological Bulletin* 134, no. 2 (April 2008): 270–300, https://www.researchgate.net/publication/5554527_The_Effects_of_Choice_on_Intrinsic_Motivation_and_Related_Outcomes_A_Meta-Analysis_of_Research_Findings.

7 Rebecca Johannsen and Paul J. Zak, "Autonomy Raises Productivity: An Experiment Measuring Neurophysiology," *Frontiers in Psychology* (May 2020), https://doi.org/10.3389/fpsyg.2020.00963.

A free ebook edition is available with the purchase of this book.

Print & Digital Together Forever.

Snap a photo   Free ebook   Read anywhere